P9-ELO-849

101 Spanish Idioms

Understanding Spanish Language and Culture Through Popular Phrases

J. M. Cassagne

Illustrated by L. N. Raidon

E. Millán, Consulting Editor

Printed on recyclable paper

PASSPORT BOOKS
a division of *NTC Publishing Group*
Lincolnwood, Illinois USA

1995 Printing

Published by Passport Books, a division of NTC Publishing Group.
© 1995 by NTC Publishing Group. 4255 West Touhy Avenue,
Lincolnwood (Chicago), Illinois 60646-1975 U.S.A.

Library of Congress Catalog Card Number: 95-68242

5 6 7 8 9 VP 9 8 7 6 5 4 3 2

Contents

en Guatepeor □ Vaciar el costal □ Bailar en la cuerda floja □ Tascar el freno □ Caer chuzos de punta □ Darle a uno una buena lejía □ Ponerse de jarras □ Tener mal templada la guitarra □ Ensartar perlas □ Hacerse un lío □ Cortarle un traje a uno

Section Five:
De todo un poco—Odds and Ends

Tener la sartén por el mango □ Quedar a la altura de su zapatilla □ Caerse del nido □ Dejar a uno en la estacada □ Subirse a la parra □ Estar entre la espada y la pared □ Cortar los lazos □ Descubrir el polvorín □ La pelota está aún en el tejado □ Empezar la casa por el tejado □ Tener telarañas en los ojos □ Saber latín

Section Six:
El planeta azul—The Blue Planet

Echar agua al mar □ Estar en las nubes □ No es cosa del otro mundo □ Todo va viento en popa □ El mundo es un pañuelo □ Tragarle a uno la tierra □ Quien no se arriesga no pasa la mar □ Como pez en el agua □ Estar entre dos aguas □ Agua pasada no mueve molino □ Parecerse como dos gotas de agua □ Mandar al quinto pino

Section Seven:
Santos y pecadores—Saints and Sinners

Un viento de mil demonios □ Alzarse con el santo y la limosna □ Andar de Herodes a Pilato □ Tener ángel □ Quedarse para vestir santos □ Hacer su santa voluntad □ Aquello fue llegar y besar el santo □ Tener el santo de espaldas □ Todos los santos tienen novena □ Más feo que el pecado

Section Eight:
Así es la vida—That's Life

Venir con músicas □ Ir por lana y volver trasquilado □ Cantar de plano □ No poder ver a alguien ni en pintura □ Fumarse una clase □ Decirle a alguien cuatro verdades □ Destornillarse de risa □ Tener un tornillo flojo □ No saber ni papa de □ Costar un ojo de la cara □ Quemarse las pestañas □ Perder los estribos □ Faltarle a uno un tornillo

Foreword

Nonnative speakers of Spanish can reach a point in their knowledge of the language where they feel comfortable with standard, formal speech. However, they're liable to get themselves in hot water when confronted with idiomatic expressions. When hearing an idiom such as *mandarle a alguien a freír espárragos* ("to have someone fry asparagus"), they may feel frustrated and confused, since the true meaning of the idiom usually cannot be determined by a knowledge of its component parts. In many cases, attempts to tie down the definition of a Spanish idiom that would work in all instances is a futile undertaking.

When native Spanish-speakers use idioms, they sound natural and suitable to the occasion, since the speakers instinctively feel the imagery and impact of what they are saying. A nonnative speaker of Spanish, on the other hand, may know the basic meaning of such expressions as *cortar el bacalao* or *tener la sartén por el mango* but still might not be able to use them appropriately. For example, if a nonnative speaker of Spanish called a leading corporation and wanted to know who was in charge by asking the receptionist "¿Quién corta el bacalao?" or "¿Quién tiene la sartén por el mango?", the chances are that the Spanish-speaking receptionist would be trying her hardest to hold back peals of laughter. Even with a fairly accurate idea of the meaning of an idiomatic expression, the nonnative lacks the intuitive feel for its impact or for the "picture" it creates.

101 Spanish Idioms is designed to bridge the gap between the *meaning* and *impact* of Spanish colloquialisms by providing a situation and a graphic illustration of that situation. In this way, the imagery created by the expression can be *felt*, rather than simply learned as a stock definition.

The book is divided into eight sections. The title of each section reflects an aspect of the natural world, the social world, or the world of the emotions—all of which the reader can easily identify with.

Both the literal and actual meanings of each expression are presented here. The presentation of the literal meaning is deliberate, since in combination with the visual element, it leads you to the imagery that gave rise to the real meaning of the phrase. A narrative or dialogue in Spanish also accompanies each expression, showing it in a natural context and, thus, further clarifying its actual meaning and use in everyday speech. Translations of the narratives and dialogues have been provided at the back of the book as a further aid to understanding.

It is hoped that the natural tone of the language in which the Spanish idiom is presented will help to convey the *feeling* of the idiom and the circumstances in which it may be used. The illustrations graphically depict the meaning of the expressions, and not only add an element of humor, but also serve to highlight the contrast between the literal and actual meanings of the idioms presented in the text.

Two indexes are included to facilitate recall and location of the expressions; one lists idioms by key images and the other lists the idioms in alphabetical order.

101 Spanish Idioms is intended for anyone who has an interest in learning more about the Spanish language and Hispanic culture. Whether you are currently studying Spanish, are planning a trip to a Spanish-speaking country, or simply want to understand the Hispanic mind better, you will find yourself referring to this collection of colorful Spanish idioms again and again.

Section One

Nuestros amigos los animales

Our Animal Friends

Cortar el bacalao

(to cut the codfish)
to rule the roost

A: ¿Has oído que van a tener que quitar todos los árboles de la plaza mayor?

B: ¿Por qué?

A: Porque la esposa del alcalde no puede ver lo que sus vecinas están haciendo en sus casas con los árboles de por medio. Entonces, para que la vieja pueda espiarlas mejor, el municipio va a quitar todos los árboles de la plaza.

B: Pero, ¿ella puede hacer eso?

A: ¡Claro que sí! Como aquí es ella quien **corta el bacalao, puede hacer lo que le dé la gana.** Lo bueno es que una vez que quiten los árboles, ¡todos podremos ver lo que está haciendo ella!

Te conozco bacalao aunque vengas disfrazado

**(I know you, codfish,
even though you're in disguise)**
I know what your little game is

A: Buenos días, Héctor. ¿Cómo está mi vecino favorito?

B: Bien, gracias. Y tú, Jorge, ¿cómo estás?

A: Estoy muy contento porque te veo más joven que nunca, Héctor.
¿Cómo lo haces? Y tu querida familia. La esposa más hermosa del
barrio, los niños más obedientes y estudiosos. Seguro que tu vida
es un sueño, Héctor. Eres el hombre más afortunado que conozco.

B: Un momento, Jorge. ¡Sólo te queda elogiar a mi perro! Mira, **te
conozco bacalao aunque vengas disfrazado.** Ya sé que tu perro
mató a mi gato y que tu esposa dañó mi carro y que tu hijo pegó al
mío. **No me vengas con más cumplidos falsos.** Es más: ¡yo siempre odiaba ese gato, el carro no es mío sino de mi cuñado, y mi hijo
se lo merecía!

2

Caerse de su burro

(to fall from your donkey)
to admit one's mistake

A: Mi vida, ¿vamos bien por esta carretera? ¡Salimos de casa hace más de tres horas y aún no hemos llegado a casa de mi mamá!

B: Claro, preciosa. Estoy tomando una ruta nueva para que podamos ver el lindo paisaje por aquí.

A: Pero mi amor, vamos hacia el sur cuando la casa de mamá queda al norte. Ve cómo se está poniendo el sol al lado derecho.

B: Es el reflejo del sol, mi corazón. Vamos al norte hacia la casa de mi adorada suegra.

A: Es que nunca **te caes de tu burro,** Luis. Sabes que vas mal, pero no **quieres reconocer tu error.** Es que no quieres visitar a mamá.

B: ¡Al contrario! Tengo tantas ganas de ver a tu mamá que estoy dispuesto a seguir esta ruta hasta que lleguemos, ¡aunque tengamos que darle la vuelta al mundo entero!

Reír con risa de conejo

(to laugh with the laughter of a rabbit)
to force a laugh

A: Hola, Pedro. ¿Es cierto que el jefe te ha nombrado vice-presidente?

B: ¡Claro que sí, Manuel! Él y yo somos muy buenos amigos ahora.

A: Pero, ¿cómo lo lograste?

B: Bueno, como el jefe piensa que es el hombre más chistoso del mundo, aprendí a reírme de sus bromas.

A: ¿Cómo es posible? ¡Él cuenta los peores chistes del mundo...y los cuenta mal!

B: Es que he aprendido a **reírme con risa de conejo,** y así él me tiene confianza. Cuando tengo que **esforzarme a reír** sólo pienso en lo ridículo que se ve así, y me salen unas risas tremendas.

Hay cuatro gatos

(there are four cats)
there's hardly a soul,
there's hardly anyone

Mi amiga Susana, autora de varias obras de teatro, me invitó a la primera función de su última obra, "Cien años de densidad", hoy, el 14 de septiembre. Cuando llegué al teatro, recibí la sorpresa de mi vida. Sólo **había cuatro gatos** en la sala. **Casi nadie había venido.** Parece que Susana es una excelente dramaturga, pero como editora de folletos promocionales, deja mucho que desear, sobre todo en cuanto a precisar la fecha de la primera función...¡el 15!

Llevarse el gato al agua

(to take the cat to the water)
to bring something off, to succeed

En un partido de fútbol contra su rival de siempre, nuestro equipo
jugó muy mal al comenzar el período. No sé qué les dijo el entrenador
durante el medio tiempo, pero cuando los chicos volvieron a jugar
la segunda mitad, **se llevaron el gato al agua** y **pudieron triunfar**
4 a 2.

Acostarse con las gallinas

(to go to bed with the hens)
to go to bed very early

A: Bueno, ya hemos cenado y apenas son las nueve de la noche.
¿Adónde vamos ahora? ¿Al cine?

B: No, yo no puedo ir a ninguna parte. Estoy muy cansada y suelo
estar dormida a estas horas.

A: No me digas que **te acuestas tan temprano.**

B: Así es. Me gusta **acostarme con las gallinas** y despertarme con el
canto de los gallos.

Largar a otro el mochuelo

(to pass the owl on to someone else)
to pass the buck

El jefe me pidió que despidiera a Juanita. No hacía su trabajo bien y alguien tenía que decírselo. Hablé con su mejor amiga, Ángela, porque **quería que ella me resolviera el problema.** Le pedí que le contara a Juanita que otra compañía estaba buscando una recepcionista y que sería mejor si ella se trasladara allá. Ángela se lo contó, y lo hizo tan bien que Juanita se fue contenta. Cuando mi jefe se enteró de todo, me llamó a su oficina.

A: Carlos, te pedí que tú hablaras con Juanita. ¿Por qué lo hizo Ángela?

B: Bueno, jefe, siempre vale **largar a otro el mochuelo,** especialmente si aquel 'otro' es la mejor amiga de la persona afectada. ¿No le parece?

A: Tienes toda la razón, Carlos. Tú tienes madera de ejecutivo, hijo.

B: Gracias, señor.

A: Y Carlos, asegúrate de que ese 'mochuelo' recibe una buena prima con su sueldo este mes...¡la que tú hubieras ganado!

Estar como boca de lobo

(to be like a wolf's mouth)
to be pitch dark

Nos guiaron por las cavernas hasta llegar muy adentro de una cueva grande. Allá el guía nos pidió que apagáramos todas las luces, y **estaba como boca de lobo.** No se podía ver nada, ni siquiera la mano frente a los ojos. Yo nunca había experimentado **una oscuridad tan absoluta** y eso me asustó un poco. Pero unos momentos después prendieron las luces y todos nos sentimos mejor.

Haberle visto las orejas al lobo

(to have seen the wolf's ears)
to have had a narrow escape, a close shave

Queríamos regalarle un perrito a nuestra hija. Llamé a un señor que había puesto un aviso en el periódico y decidimos encontrarnos esa noche en el estacionamiento de un restaurante cerrado. Cuando llegué, él ya estaba vendiéndole un perro a un joven. Noté que se había estacionado en la parte más oscura del estacionamiento y empecé a tener mis dudas. Al ver el perrito que el joven había comprado, me di cuenta de que el pobre animal tenía sarna, pero no se la podía notar bien debido a la oscuridad. Nos fuimos sin hablar con el tipo porque ya **le habíamos visto las orejas al lobo. Por poco nos engaña,** pero vimos la trampa justamente a tiempo.

Encomendar
las ovejas al lobo

(to entrust the sheep to the wolf)
to put the fox in charge
of the henhouse

A: Manolo, ven aquí. Nos vamos al dentista.

B: Pero mamá, no quiero ir. Mi novia está aquí y no quiero dejarla sola.

A: Que se quede con tu hermano. Él puede conversar con ella mientras tanto. Nos vamos.

B: Pero no comprendes, mamá. Eso sería como **encomendar las ovejas al lobo.** Juan quiere robármela. No puedo **dejarla en sus manos así.**

A: Bueno, entonces dile a Juan que vaya al dentista, y tú te quedas en casa. Al fin y al cabo, ya que tienes novia es mejor que no te veas más con esa chica que le ayuda al Dr. Soto.

B: Un momentito, mamá. Tal vez debo tratar de tener más confianza en Juan...

Sacudir la mosca

(to shake off the fly)
to cough up the dough

A: Pedro, ¿por qué andas tan triste?

B: Bueno, acabo de encontrarme con Javier. Hacía ya tiempo que me había prestado dinero y hoy me dijo que **sacudiera la mosca** inmediatamente.

A: Hombre, eso me parece justo.

B: Pero me molestó **darle la plata** porque pensaba comprarle un buen regalo de cumpleaños a mi novia. Después de pagarle a Javier, me he quedado sin nada.

No oír ni el vuelo
de una mosca

(to not even hear the flight of a fly)
you could have heard a pin drop

Les dije a los nuevos estudiantes que no hablaran durante el examen, pero no esperaba el **absoluto silencio** que mantuvieron durante los 50 minutos del examen. **No se oía ni el vuelo de una mosca.** Quedé bien impresionada y decidí decirles que estudiaran español tres horas diarias a ver si eso tendría el mismo resultado.

¡A otro perro con ese hueso!

(to another dog with that bone!)
don't give me that! come off it!

A: Buenos días, señor. ¡Tengo el gusto de comunicarle que usted
puede ser ganador de un millón de pesos!

B: ¿Cómo?

A: Es muy sencillo. Cuando usted compre este magnífico juego de
enciclopedias, incluimos su nombre en nuestro gran sorteo para
ganar un millón de pesos. Sólo tiene que firmar...

B: **¡A otro perro con ese hueso! No me va a engañar con ese truco.**
No necesito enciclopedias. Buenos días.

Darle perro a uno

(to give someone a dog)
to stand someone up, break a date

A: Luis, ¿qué haces con esas flores en la mano?

B: Estoy esperando a Carla. Me invitó a cenar y dijo que pasaría por mí a las siete, pero ya son las nueve.

A: Creo que **te dio perro.** Ella es siempre muy puntual. Seguro que **no vendrá para la cita.** Tal vez se encontró con otro chico más guapo, ¿no crees?

B: ¡Gracias por animarme tanto!

Pagar el pato

(to pay for the duck)
to pay for someone else's mistakes, to get railroaded

Hubo un tremendo escándalo el mes pasado. Parece que el Ministro de Transporte recibía sobornos de una compañía de autobuses para que él les diera contratos gordos. Le regalaron un yate y mucho dinero, pero cuando la policía empezó a investigar el asunto, fue el Director de Ferrocarriles quien tuvo que **pagar el pato.** El yate "apareció" detrás de su casa una mañana y él **fue declarado culpable** en todos los periódicos. El director insistió en que casi se marea bañándose en la tina. Según él, ni sabe navegar, pero no se lo creyeron y fue destituido de su puesto. Unos días después, la casa del Ministro fue destruida por una bomba. Nunca hallaron al culpable, ¡pero alguien dejó un ancla donde había estado la tina del Ministro!

Arrimar uno el ascua a su sardina

(to draw the embers next to one's sardine)
to look out for number one

Dos investigadores médicos trabajaron por años en un proyecto para encontrar una droga que curara la obesidad. Isabel, la tímida genio del laboratorio, descubrió la fórmula para crear la droga, pero Jorge, su extrovertido colega, la fabricó y la promocionó. Cuando los representantes del comité Nobel entrevistaron a Jorge en cuanto a su gran descubrimiento, **él arrimó el ascua a su sardina.** Ni siquiera mencionó a Isabel. Aceptó todas sus felicitaciones como si lo hubiera hecho solo, **aprovechándose de la situación.** Seis meses después, cuando los pacientes empezaron a quejarse de que se les estaba cayendo el pelo, Jorge insistió en que la fórmula era de Isabel, pero nadie se lo creía y fue arruinado en los círculos científicos. Más tarde, Isabel perfeccionó la fórmula y llegó a ser multimillonaria. Jorge actualmente es su chofer.

Cuando las ranas críen pelo

(when frogs grow hair)
when pigs fly

A: Nuestro equipo de fútbol es pésimo. Nunca ganaremos ni un solo partido.

B: No seas tan pesimista. De pronto tendremos suerte contra algún equipo malísimo y ganaremos.

A: Tendría que ser un equipo de ciegos. Si no, creo que ganaremos un partido **cuando las ranas críen pelo,** ¿no te parece?

B: Puede que tengas razón. Tal vez **nunca** ganemos pero, ¿quién sabe? A lo mejor nos toca el campeonato en el torneo de jubilados dentro de treinta años...¡jugamos como viejos ya!

Section Two

Hablando del cuerpo . . .

Speaking About the Body . . .

Tener el corazón hecho pedazos

(to have one's heart turned into pieces)
to be heartbroken,
to be broken-hearted

A: Hola, Pepito. ¿Por qué lloras?

B: Es que mamá se fue de viaje por una semana entera y la echo de menos. Por eso **estoy tan triste.**

A: Pero no debes **tener el corazón hecho pedazos** sólo porque ella no estará aquí por una semana. Pronto volverá y va a preguntarme cómo te portaste. ¿Qué quieres que le diga...que pasaste toda la semana llorando como un chiquillo o que te portaste como un mayorcito?

B: Bueno, si eso va a hacer que ella no haga más viajes así, ¡puedes decirle que mis lágrimas causaron un verdadero diluvio!

Caérsele a uno las alas del corazón

(to lose the wings of one's heart)
to become discouraged

Ana se quedó sin trabajo el año pasado. No se preocupó porque tenía buena formación, mucha experiencia y excelente entrenamiento en su campo de trabajo. Contestó muchos avisos del periódico, fue a varias entrevistas, pero nada resultó. Después de seis meses de buscar empleo sin éxito, **se le están cayendo las alas del corazón.** Es bastante difícil encontrar un buen trabajo estos días. Le puede **desanimar** a cualquiera. Espero que consiga algo pronto o va a tener que aceptar algún trabajo mediocre sólo para sobrevivir.

Coger a alguien con las manos en la masa

(to catch someone with his or her hands in the dough)
to catch someone red-handed

La policía ya tenía sus sospechas acerca de Enrique en cuanto a unos robos armados en el barrio, pero no pudieron **cogerlo con las manos en la masa.** Un día, un joven policía se disfrazó de vendedor en una joyería. Cuando Enrique entró en la tienda y sacó un cuchillo para robar al vendedor, el policía sacó su pistola y llevó a Enrique a la cárcel. Lo había pillado **en el acto** del robo.

Llenar la cabeza de pajaritos

(to fill the head with little birds)
to fill someone's head with empty talk

Por televisión, por radio, en los periódicos y revistas, nos bombardean de mensajes comerciales. Cada compañía promete más que la anterior en cuanto a la felicidad, el éxito y la popularidad que su producto nos garantizará. Pero después de escuchar sus gritos, ver sus fotos y oír sus promociones, a menudo nos parece que nos quieren **llenar la cabeza de pajaritos.** Seguro que sus productos no son tan mágicos como los pintan. Es que nos quieren **convencer con argumentos vacíos** que no tienen sentido. ¿Usar esa crema de afeitar te hace más atractivo? ¿Llevar cierta colonia te hace más romántica? ¿Usar una crema de dientes especial te convierte en el mejor amante del mundo? ¡Lo dudo! Son promesas imposibles de cumplir.

Hinchársele
las narices a alguien

(to make someone's nostrils flare)
to make someone lose his or her temper, to get someone's dander up

A: Paco, ¿por qué sigues molestándome? Te dije que no quiero jugar al tenis hoy. Deja de pegarme con esa raqueta.

B: Pero no hay nadie más, José. Tienes que jugar. O pego la pelota en un partido contigo o te pego a ti.

A: Paco, te digo que **me estás hinchando las narices.** Deja de **molestarme** o te voy a echar esta magnífica limonada en la cara.

B: Bueno, bueno, viejo. No tienes que ponerte así. Si no quieres jugar, basta con decírmelo.

Dar en un hueso

(to hit a bone)
to hit a snag

A: Camilo, ¿mi televisor ya está reparado?

B: No, don Alonso. Lo siento.

A: Pero prometiste tenerlo listo hoy.

B: Sí, yo sé, pero **di en un hueso,** don Alonso. La pieza no me llegó.

A: ¿Por qué no?

B: Bueno, es que mi cuñado me trae las piezas y él es muy perezoso, señor. Él es la razón por la que **tengo todas estas demoras inesperadas.**

A: ¿Por qué no lo despides?

B: Patrón, es que mi esposa dice que si él no tiene trabajo, tiene que venir a vivir en casa con nosotros, ¡y eso sí que no aguanto!

Hablar con el corazón en la mano

(to speak with one's heart in one's hand)
to speak from the heart

A: Enrique, eres mi mejor amigo. Quiero pedirte un consejo. Sabes que soy tímido, especialmente cuando se trata de hablar con las mujeres. Conozco a una hermosa y encantadora mujer llamada Alicia. Nos conocimos hace tres semanas y creo que la quiero, pero no sé cómo decírselo. ¿Qué debo hacer?

B: Creo que lo mejor sería **hablarle con el corazón en la mano,** Jaime. Si estás seguro de lo que sientes por ella, debes **decírselo franca y abiertamente.** Puede que ella sienta lo mismo por ti.

Ponérsele la mosca detrás de la oreja

(to put the fly behind someone's ear)
to have one's suspicions aroused

Algo raro me pasó ayer. Iba caminando por la calle cuando un individuo se me acercó y me preguntó si quería comprar un reloj. Le pregunté, <<¿Qué reloj?>>, y él subió la manga de su saco para mostrarme unos veinte relojes que llevaba en el brazo. Inmediatamente, **se me puso la mosca detrás de la oreja.** Y cuando me dijo que todos estaban al precio especial de sólo diez dólares, **mis sospechas** se confirmaron. En eso, pasó un policía que le vio los relojes y trató de arrestarlo. El hombre se fue corriendo. ¡Menos mal que yo no estaba comprando uno de esos relojes cuando llegó el policía!

No llegarle a uno al tobillo

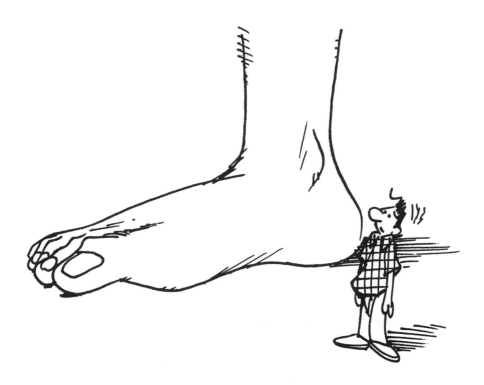

(not to come up to anybody's ankle)
not to be able to hold a candle to anyone

A: ¿Qué piensas de nuestro nuevo boxeador, "Alex el Asesino?"

B: ¡Es magnífico! Nunca he visto a nadie que **le llegue al tobillo** siquiera. Él es el mejor.

A: Sí, **es el mejor** que conozco, pero no he visto al cubano. Lo llaman "Miguel el Matón."

B: Sí, pero pronto lo van a llamar "Miguel el Muerto" cuando Alex termine con él.

Tomarle el pelo a uno

(to pull someone's hair)
to pull someone's leg

A: Ayer era el día de los inocentes y nos divertimos muchísimo con Juan, el campeón de natación.

B: ¿Verdad? ¿Qué le hicieron?

A: Sabes que Juan nunca deja pasar ni un solo día sin nadar en el mar. Dice que es su "compromiso de campeón." Está muy orgulloso de sus logros. Entonces le dijimos que unos marineros habían visto un tiburón en la bahía.

B: ¡Ay, pero **le estaban tomando el pelo!** ¿No se dio cuenta de que **estaban bromeando?**

A: Creo que no. En todo caso, lo escuchamos cuando le dijo a su novia que no iba a nadar mañana porque sufría unos calambres fuertes y quería dejar que los músculos descansaran unos días. ¡Nos reímos como locos!

Section Three

Algo en
que pensar

Food for Thought

Buscarle pelos al huevo

(to look for hair on the egg)
to nitpick, to find fault with everything

A: Buenos días. ¿Está listo mi carro?

B: Sí, señor, y hemos arreglado todo...los frenos, las llantas, el acelerador y el cambio de aceite.

A: ¿Qué tipo de llantas me dieron...las XB normales o las JX especiales?

B: Las especiales, señor, como usted dijo.

A: Y los frenos...¿me los apretaron muy bien?

B: Sí, señor, como usted dijo.

A: Y cuando arreglaron el acelerador... ¿le pusieron un cable normal o uno con acero reforzado?

B: Francamente señor, hay poca diferencia. Son iguales.

A: ¡No me digas que usaron el cable normal! No puedo tolerar la incompetencia. ¿Por qué no usaron el de acero?

B: Señor, creo que usted está **buscándole pelos al huevo** en esto.

A: Puede ser, pero siempre me gusta **prestar atención a los detalles.**

Andar pisando huevos

(to walk stepping on eggs)
to tread on thin ice

A: ¿Cómo resultaron las negociaciones, señora Embajadora?

B: Bueno, nos fue muy bien hasta que uno de mis asistentes se equivocó y mencionó los problemas de la frontera entre nuestros países. Como **es un asunto muy delicado,** por poco cancelan todo.

A: ¿Qué pudo hacer, señora Embajadora, para rescatar la reunión?

B: Fue difícil. Yo tenía que **andar pisando huevos** por un tiempo, pero pronto se calmaron y pudimos seguir con las negociaciones.

Poner toda la carne
en el asador

(to put all the meat on the spit)
to put everything into it, to put all
your eggs in one basket

Luisa escribió un guión de cine muy bueno titulado "Las estrellas de la tarde". Se lo presentó a todas las grandes compañías cinematográficas americanas, pero sin éxito. El trabajo le había costado mucho dinero por los vuelos de ciudad en ciudad y las noches en hoteles, y no le quedaba mucho. Pero Luisa tenía tanta confianza en su guión que decidió **poner toda la carne en el asador** y producir la película ella misma. **Gastó todo lo que tenía** y consiguió préstamos, pero la película tuvo muchísimo éxito.

Llamar al pan
pan y al vino vino

(to call bread bread and wine wine)
to call a spade a spade

A: Buenos días, señora directora. ¿Me pidió venir a la escuela para...?

B: Para hablar de su hijo, señora Castellón. Tenemos problemas con él. Resulta que encontramos dinero de otro estudiante en la chaqueta de su hijo. No estamos seguros pero...

A: Señora, **llamemos al pan pan y al vino vino.** ¿Está usted diciendo que mi hijo es un ladrón?

B: Sí, señora Castellón, **seamos francas.** Pensamos que su hijo cometió un robo.

Hacer buenas
migas con alguien

(to make good crumbs with someone)
to get along well with someone,
to hit it off

A: ¿Qué tal, Alejandro? ¿Cómo va todo?

B: Tenemos otro jefe aquí ahora. El señor Gómez se jubiló.

A: ¡Qué lástima! Ustedes dos eran muy buenos amigos, ¿cierto?

B: Sí, y lo echo de menos, pero creo que el nuevo jefe va a ser bueno
también. **Hago buenas migas con él.**

A: ¡Qué bien! Siempre vale la pena **tener buenas relaciones** con
el jefe.

Estar hasta en la sopa

(to be even in the soup)
there is no getting away from someone

A: ¿Has oído lo de la famosa actriz a quien acusan de haber matado a su director?

B: Claro que sí. Hablan del caso en todos los programas de noticias, en todos los programas de entrevistas, y hasta proyectan sus viejas películas todas las noches. **¡Está hasta en la sopa!**

A: Eso es cierto. Estoy harto de escuchar de ella día y noche. **Aparece en todas partes.**

Mandarle a alguien a freír espárragos

(to have someone fry asparagus)
to tell someone to go jump in the lake

Ese Francisco me está volviendo loco. Viene a mi oficina cada media hora para hablar de alguna bobada personal. Esta mañana vino a las nueve para hablar de su suegra, a las nueve y media para hablar de su carro, a las diez para hablar de sus hijos y a las diez y media para hablar de su perro. Cuando llegó otra vez a las once, perdí la paciencia y **le mandé a freír espárragos.** Es que no puedo aguantar más interrupciones en mi trabajo. Por eso **le dije que se largara.**

Sacar las castañas
del fuego a alguien

(to pull the chestnuts
out of the fire for someone)
to save someone's neck

El capitán mandó al sargento Molino y al cabo Gómez a la jungla para una misión peligrosa. El sargento Molino dio todas las órdenes pero el cabo Gómez hizo todo el trabajo. Gómez cortó la hierba para abrir el camino y construyó un puente para cruzar el río. Cuando aparecieron dos culebras, las mató Gómez y cuando un tigre salió de la jungla fue Gómez quien tuvo que espantarlo. Y al final fue Gómez quien destruyó la fortificación del enemigo. Fue el cabo Gómez quien **había sacado las castañas del fuego a Molino.**

Cuando llegaron a la oficina del teniente, Molino recibió todas las felicitaciones por la misión cumplida y ni siquiera mencionó a Gómez, quien **había hecho todo el trabajo.**

Llevarse calabazas

(to carry off pumpkins)
to lose

A: Oye, ¿qué son los resultados de la elección? ¿Fue elegida de nuevo la alcaldesa Santiago?

B: Tengo los resultados ya y a la alcaldesa **se llevó calabazas.** Ella **perdió** por casi dos mil votos.

A: ¿Y cuántos votaron?

B: Unos dos mil trescientos.

No partir peras con nadie

(not to share pears with anyone)
to act alone in one's own interest,
to go out on one's own

Cuando yo tenía veinte años empecé un grupo de jazz con unos amigos. Nos llamamos "Los Jazzmen." Presentamos conciertos por todo México con mucho éxito, pero un día, Álvaro, el guitarrista, nos anunció que había decidido **no partir peras con nadie.** Nos dejó para hacer una carrera independiente como solista.

Hoy, "Los Jazzmen" somos famosos en toda América Latina, pero Álvaro es todavía un desconocido. A veces no vale **obrar aisladamente y tratar de triunfar solo.**

Echar leña al fuego

(to throw wood on the fire)
to add fuel to the fire

Cuando Alberto llegó a la casa de Marcos y Marina, éstos ya estaban peleando. Alberto escuchó mientras Marcos le acusaba a Marina de ser una aguafiestas que nunca quiere salir de casa y Marina le acusaba a Marcos de siempre querer salir con lo suyo. Alberto, en vez de marcharse, decidió **echar leña al fuego.** Comentó que estaba de acuerdo con Marcos, y luego lo invitó al cine. Marina se puso furiosa y le echó a Alberto de la casa con una patada bien fuerte. Es que a veces no conviene **empeorar una discusión fuerte** entre esposos, especialmente si la esposa es más fuerte que uno.

Ir al grano

(to go to the seed)
to get to the point

A: Hola, papá. Estás elegantísimo con esa nueva camisa. Ese color te favorece. ¿O será que has perdido peso? Estás muy guapo.

B: Gracias, hija.

A: Papá, mis amigas no tienen tanta suerte como yo. Sus padres no son tan cariñosos y generosos como tú. Ninguno de ellos quiere llevarnos al cine esta tarde...

B: Bueno, hijita, deja de decir bobadas. Si quieres pedirme que las lleve al cine, debes **ir al grano,** y decírmelo.

A: Vale. Papá, ¿nos llevas al cine esta tarde?

B: **En una palabra,** Alicia: ¡NO!

Section Four

En las buenas y en las malas

For Better or Worse

La última gota que hace rebosar la copa

(the last drop that makes the glass overflow)
the last straw

A: Mamá, quiero ir al parque...vámonos...por favor, por favor...

B: ¡Basta ya! De acuerdo. Iremos al parque, pero ponte la chaqueta. Hace frío hoy.

A: ¡No quiero ponerme la chaqueta! No me la pongo, no me gusta.

B: Está bien, pero no seas tan llorón.

A: *[EN EL PARQUE]* Mamá, tengo frío. ¡Ah! ¡Cuánto frío tengo! Me muero de frío. Déjame tu chaqueta, mamá.

B: ¡Eso **es el colmo** y **la última gota que hace rebosar la copa!** Nos vamos a casa inmediatamente. Y la próxima vez que te digo que te pongas la chaqueta, te la pones o no salimos de casa.

41

Ponerse las botas

(to put one's boots on)
to make a killing

Isabel estaba de vacaciones en una bonita playa de México. Como era el mes de julio, hacía un calor insoportable. A Isabel le entró muchísima sed, pero no había ningún lugar en toda la playa donde comprar refrescos. En ese momento, tuvo la idea de abrir un pequeño puesto donde la gente podría tomar algo frío. Pronto el puesto "Doña Isabelita" se convirtió en el centro de gravedad de la playa. Isabel tuvo muchísimo éxito y **se puso las botas.** Como no tenía competencia, **se llenó los bolsillos de plata.**

Estar de veinticinco alfileres

(to be of twenty-five pins)
to be dressed to kill

Los Fernández me invitaron a su casa el otro día. Como ellos viven en el campo y la fiesta era un domingo de verano por la tarde, pensé que todos irían con ropa deportiva. Me puse unos vaqueros, una camisa de manga corta, mis zapatos de tenis y fui a su casa. ¡Qué vergüenza! Cuando entré me di cuenta de que era una reunión muy elegante. Todos los invitados **estaban de veinticinco alfileres.** Los hombres llevaban trajes hechos a la medida y corbata, y las señoras llevaban vestidos elegantísimos e iban cubiertas de joyas carísimas. Todos **iban bien vestidos** menos yo. ¡Lo pasé fatal!

Salir de Guatemala y meterse en Guatepeor

(to leave "Guate-bad" and go into "Guate-worse")
to go from bad to worse, out of the frying pan into the fire

Los dos presos no aguantaron más ni su falta de libertad ni su pequeña y maloliente celda. Decidieron cavar un túnel de escape. Trabajaron todas las noches durante tres semanas. Por fin llegó la hora de cavar la última parte del túnel y escaparse, pero cuando salieron del túnel, se dieron cuenta de que **habían salido de Guatemala y se metieron en Guatepeor.** En vez de salir de la cárcel, el túnel los llevó a la celda de castigo, ¡el único lugar de toda la prisión que **era peor** que su celda!

Vaciar el costal

(to empty the bag)
to get it off one's chest

Mi vecino me tiene loco. Constantemente me pide prestadas cosas que jamás devuelve, su perro estropea todas mis flores, su gato ataca a mis canarios y su hijo anda pegando al mío. Por fin decidí **decirle exactamente lo que pensaba de él** y de toda su familia. No sé qué me había impedido **vaciarle el costal** mucho antes, pero cuando el vecino abrió la puerta, de repente recordé por qué no lo había hecho. Él mide dos metros y tiene brazos como de gorila. Le balbuceé que había olvidado por qué había venido y me fui.

Bailar en la cuerda floja

(to dance on the slack rope)
to walk the tightrope, to be on the razor's edge

A: Marta, ¿cómo va tu nuevo negocio?

B: No muy bien, Jorge. La competencia entre heladerías aquí en la playa es feroz. No sé qué me va a pasar.

A: Pero, ¿ganas suficiente para cubrir tus gastos y pagar la nota en el banco?

B: Pues no. **Estoy bailando en la cuerda floja,** Jorge. Estoy a punto de declararme en bancarrota en cualquier momento. ¿Quieres ayudarme? Podrías ser mi socio.

A: No, gracias, Marta, yo sólo quería saber cómo te va, no quiero unirme a tu **situación precaria.**

Tascar el freno

(to hit the brakes)
to show impatience,
to champ at the bit

El señor Borges necesitaba alguien que le ayudara en la administración de la empresa, y Lisa tenía grandes esperanzas de ser la asistente que él buscaba. Ella sabía que sería perfecta para ese puesto y quería decírselo al señor Borges cuando éste anunció que su hijo iba a ocupar el puesto. Desde entonces, Lisa **tasca el freno. Está impaciente** por conseguir otra oportunidad de ascenso.

Caer chuzos de punta

(to rain sharp-pointed spears)
to rain cats and dogs

A: Vicente, necesito papas. Vete a la tienda y cómprame dos kilos.

B: Pero, mamá, ¡**caen chuzos de punta!**

A: Lleva el paraguas.

B: Pero **llueve muy fuerte.** Aún con paraguas voy a mojarme mucho. Voy a esperar unos minutos a que escampe.

A: Está bien, pero no esperes demasiado. Necesito esas papas para la cena.

Darle a uno una buena lejía

(to give someone a good dose of bleach)
to give someone a good scolding

Guillermo es conductor de camiones y lleva madera de una ciudad a otra. Ayer, su jefe lo esperaba a las seis de la tarde porque tenía otro cargamento urgente que enviar a las siete. Pero a Guillermo no le importan mucho los horarios. Demoró por el camino y no llegó hasta las nueve de la noche. Basta decir que su jefe **le dio una buena lejía. Lo criticó,** diciéndole que era irresponsable, perezoso y negligente. Le dijo a Guillermo que si esto volviera a pasar, lo tendría que despedir.

Ponerse de jarras

(to put oneself like pitchers)
to put your hands on your hips, arms akimbo

Como Lolita cumplió catorce años hace poco, les preguntó a sus padres si ya podría ir al centro con sus amigos los sábados por la noche. Le dieron permiso para salir bajo la condición de que volviera a casa antes de la medianoche. Lolita les prometió que sí, y se fue tan contenta. Pero a Lolita se le olvidó la hora y cuando miró su reloj, ya eran las dos de la mañana. Cuando abrió la puerta de su casa, ¡se encontró con su padre, **puesto de jarras,** con la cara roja y humo saliendo de ambas orejas! Ahora, Lolita se queda en casa los sábados recordando a su padre **con los puños en las caderas,** cuando ella llegó tan tarde.

Tener mal templada la guitarra

(to have one's guitar badly tuned)
to be in a bad mood

A: ¿Qué pasa con el jefe hoy? Llegó a la oficina enfurecido esta mañana. Le pegó un par de gritos al mensajero, criticó severamente a la recepcionista y echó una bronca a su asistente.

B: Creo que **tiene mal templada la guitarra** porque no le dieron el aumento que pidió.

A: Seguro que es por eso, pero su **mal humor** no justifica ese comportamiento.

Ensartar perlas

(to string pearls)
to waste one's time

A: Gracias, Sra. Miller, por venir desde tan lejos para finalizar los detalles del contrato. Se lo agradezco muchísimo. ¿Quiere otro café? ¿Y cómo está su esposo? ¿Y sus ni...?

B: Perdone la interrupción, señor Ocampo, pero no vine aquí para **ensartar perlas.** Como usted, tengo mucho que hacer y poco tiempo. De manera que ¿podemos hablar del contrato ya?

A: Señora Miller, usted no está en su país ahora. Está con nosotros, y aquí no somos de la opinión de que pasar tiempo en una charla agradable antes de entrar en negociaciones sea **perder el tiempo.** Al contrario, nos parece que el estilo brusco de realizar negocios es una gran falta de cortesía.

B: Perdóneme, señor Ocampo. Parece que tengo mucho que aprender. ¿Cómo está su familia?

Hacerse un lío

(to make oneself a mess)
to make a mess of things

A: ¿Cómo van tus casos, Carlitos, o debo decir, señor abogado?

B: Mi primer caso fue horrible. Me presenté ante una juez del juzgado municipal. Me había preparado bien, pero me puse tan nervioso al hablar que **me hice un lío. Confundí todo.**

A: ¿Y a tu cliente? ¿Cómo le fue?

B: Bueno, a pesar de la confusión total en la que me metí, la juez no lo condenó, así que no tuvo que ir a la cárcel. Pero ella me advertió que me preparara mejor para el próximo caso.

Cortarle un traje a uno

(to tailor a suit for someone)
to run someone down, put them down

Ese Javier es un hipócrita total. Hace dos días, habló maravillas de Esteban mientras éste estaba presente, pero tan pronto como Esteban salió, Javier empezó a **cortarle un traje.** Dijo que era antipático, aburrido y mentiroso. Pero es cómo es—Javier siempre **habla mal** de los demás cuando no están.

Section Five

De todo un poco

Odds and Ends

Tener la sartén por el mango

(to have the frying pan by the handle)
to run the show

A: Pepe, ¿qué haces?

B: Estoy cambiando el aceite del carro de la señora Ortega.

A: Pero yo te dije que arreglaras el carro del señor Jiménez primero. Se lo prometí para esta tarde.

B: Es que la señora Ortega me pidió que hiciera su trabajo ahora porque tiene mucha prisa.

A: Mira, Pepe, aquí soy yo quien **tiene la sartén por el mango,** no la señora Ortega. Haz lo que te digo.

B: Bien, **¡usted es el que manda!**

Quedar a la altura de su zapatilla

(to remain at the height of one's slipper)
to be a failure

El sábado pasado, nuestro candidato para alcalde, Luis, nos invitó a una comida en el campo para agradecernos todo el trabajo que le habíamos hecho. Nos invitó para la una de la tarde, y nos dijo que él se encargaría de todo. Bueno, todos llegamos a la una, pero no estaba Luis. Cuando por fin llegó dos horas más tarde, se disculpó diciendo que había tenido una reunión importante y se había olvidado de la comida. No trajo absolutamente nada para comer y se marchó en seguida. Todos pensábamos que Luis **quedaba a la altura de su zapatilla.** Si **no es capaz** de organizar una comida, ¿cómo sería de alcalde? Ese día muchísima gente perdió confianza en Luis, y unos días más tarde, perdió las elecciones.

Caerse del nido

(to fall out of the nest)
to be completely surprised,
you don't say!

A: Oye, Miguel, ¡tengo noticias increíbles!

B: ¿De qué, Pablo?

A: ¿Conoces a Esperanza?

B: Claro que la conozco. Se casa con mi primo en junio.

A: Pero ella no se casa con nadie en junio, ¡porque ayer se casó con su profesor de matemáticas!

B: **¡Me caigo del nido!** No sabía nada de eso. **¡Qué sorpresa!** ¿Pero quién se lo va a decir a mi primo?

Dejar a uno en la estacada

(to leave someone in the stockade)
to leave someone in the lurch

¡Ese Pedro es el colmo! Nunca puedo confiar en él. Siempre me falla.
Quedó en reunirse conmigo aquí en la estación de tren a las dos. Él
tiene los boletos y todos los expedientes para la reunión, pero **me
dejó en la estacada** de nuevo. Ya salió el tren y no hay otro hasta
mañana. Perderemos la reunión y no habrá posibilidad de conseguir
el contrato porque Pedro **no ha cumplido con lo que había
prometido.** Voy a tener que buscar otro socio.

Subirse a la parra

(to climb up the grapevine)
to blow one's top, hit the ceiling

Tengo un colega que se pone furioso muy fácilmente. Si no está de acuerdo con algo, explota. La semana pasada le dije que no podía aprobar su plan de trabajo porque iba a pasar demasiado tiempo fuera de la oficina. **Se subió a la parra. Se puso tan bravo** que no podía ni hablar y se fue de mi oficina con la cara tan roja que un amigo lo llama "tomate" ahora cada vez que lo ve...y ¡eso lo enfurece también!

Estar entre la espada y la pared

(to be between the sword and the wall)
to be caught between a rock and a hard place

Tengo un gran problema. Mis hijos me pidieron que los llevara al zoológico el sábado. Sin pensarlo dos veces, les dije que sí. Pero después, mi marido me recordó que había prometido acompañarlo a una galería de arte. **Me encuentro entre dos opciones difíciles.** Si voy al zoológico, quedo mal con mi marido; y si voy a la galería, mis hijos se echan a llorar. No sé qué hacer. **Estoy entre la espada y la pared.**

Cortar los lazos

(to cut the bows)
to cut off all contact

A: ¿Has visto al hijo del señor Sánchez?

B: No, y no creo que lo veamos durante mucho tiempo.

A: ¿Por qué? ¿Qué pasó?

B: El joven quería ir a Hollywood para ser actor, pero su papá no quiso ayudarle. Su madre lo apoyaba, pero el señor Sánchez se opuso a la idea. Por fin el muchacho se cansó de esperar tanto y decidió **cortar los lazos** con su padre, y se fue. Creo que ya **ni se ven ni siquiera se hablan** desde aquel día.

Descubrir el polvorín

(to discover the gunpowder)
to uncover the secret

El caso de Eduardo era un enigma para la profesora de física.
Eduardo nunca estudiaba para su clase, jamás contestaba a ninguna
pregunta en clase y nunca entregaba las tareas, pero cada vez que
daba un examen, Eduardo sacaba la mejor nota. Un día la profesora
resolvió por fin **el gran misterio.** Encontró a Eduardo leyendo notas
de la manga de su camisa durante el examen. Al **descubrir el polvorín,** la profesora lo echó de la clase y a Eduardo le suspendieron la
asignatura.

La pelota está aún en el tejado

(the ball is still on the roof)
the game isn't over yet

A: No sé qué debo hacer, Manuel. He invitado a Carmen a salir conmigo dos veces ya y siempre tiene una excusa. ¿Será que no le
caigo bien?

B: Recuerda, muchacho, **la pelota está aún en el tejado.** Tengo enten-
dido que le caes muy bien y que estará libre este sábado. **No te des
por vencido.** No la has perdido todavía.

Empezar la casa por el tejado

(to start building the house at the roof)
to put the cart before the horse

A: Jaime, ¡mira mi carro!

B: ¡Es una maravilla! ¿Cuándo lo compraste?

A: Ayer.

B: Bueno, llévame a casa.

A: No puedo. No tengo licencia.

B: No tienes licencia, pero sí tienes carro. ¿Eso no es **empezar la casa por el tejado?**

A: Sé que tengo **todo fuera de orden,** pero estaban vendiendo el carro a un precio fantástico. Así que lo compré...sin licencia. Pronto aprenderé a conducir y te llevo de paseo.

Tener telarañas en los ojos

(to have cobwebs in one's eyes)
to be blind

A: Esta película me gustó, sobre todo la gran escena cuando la multitud de la antigua Roma se alborota contra los soldados.

B: Sí, fue una lucha impresionante. ¿Te fijaste en que los extras reclutados para formar la multitud todavía llevaban sus zapatos de tenis?

A: Pues no.

B: Hombre, **tendrás telarañas en los ojos. Nunca ves nada.**

Saber latín

(to know Latin)
to be nobody's fool

Luisa había dejado sus llaves dentro del coche y no quería pagarle a un cerrajero. Como la mujer **sabe latín,** llamó anónimamente a la policía y les dijo que había una bomba en un coche sospechoso (¡que por supuesto era el suyo!). Llegaron dos especialistas y consiguieron abrir la puerta. En ese momento, aparece Luisa y les pregunta qué estaban haciendo. **Ella se creía muy lista** hasta que uno de los policías vio sus llaves en el coche y se dio cuenta de lo que había pasado.

Section Six

El planeta azul

The Blue Planet

Echar agua al mar

(to throw water into the sea)
to be pointless

Ayer hacía mucho calor y llevé a los niños a la playa. Como querían cobrarme cinco dólares en el aparcamiento, decidí dejar el carro en la playa para ahorrar el dinero. Mis hijos y yo lo pasamos muy bien, pero cuando íbamos a salir, las llantas del carro se hundieron en la arena. Les pedí a los chicos que empujaran el carro mientras yo trataba de sacarlo, pero era como **echar agua al mar. No sirvió para nada.** Por fin tuve que llamar a la grúa, ¡y "el aparcamiento" me costó cincuenta dólares!

Estar en las nubes

(to be in the clouds)
to be daydreaming

A: ¿Qué va a hacer tu hija después de graduarse del colegio?

B: No sé. Ella habla de viajar por el mundo, escribir una novela o tal vez llegar a ser actriz.

A: Pero **no es muy realista.** Parece que **está en las nubes.** Mi hija, al contrario, ya se ha matriculado en la universidad para estudiar medicina. Quiere ser médica y creo que lo logrará. Es muy práctica.

No es cosa del otro mundo

(it's not anything from another world)
it's nothing to write home about

A: ¿Qué tal tu nuevo trabajo, Paco? Me han dicho que tienes un puesto importantísimo en una editorial de gran prestigio.

B: Bueno, el puesto sí es importante, pero el trabajo **va fatal.** Trabajo más horas que nunca—ni tengo tiempo para salir a comer, mi jefe está como una cabra, se me han ido dos empleados y tardo más de dos horas en llegar a la oficina. En fin, **no es cosa del otro mundo.**

Todo va viento en popa

(everything goes wind at the stern)
all is going well

Gloria Castro es la nueva estrella de la canción sudamericana. Su reciente éxito, "Dame tu amor", ha vendido millones de discos. Los periódicos y las revistas hablan de ella constantemente. En este momento, se puede decir que **todo le va viento en popa.** Espero que muy pronto pueda grabar otra canción y así **seguir teniendo éxito** en su carrera.

El mundo es un pañuelo

(the world is a handkerchief)
it's a small world

El año pasado fui a una isla solitaria en medio del Pacífico. Había estado trabajando muchísimo y necesitaba escaparme de la oficina y de la rutina diaria. Me apetecía descansar en la playa, con la sola compañía de un par de buenos libros. ¡Qué sorpresa me llevé cuando descubrí que en el mismo hotel donde me quedaba, estaban no sólo unos vecinos míos, sino el contable de la oficina y su mujer, mi dentista, la directora de la agencia de viajes, su marido y sus cinco hijos! Como decía mi abuela: **¡El mundo es un pañuelo!** Demasiado pequeño para mi gusto—la isla paradisiaca se había convertido en **algo familiar y casi rutinario.**

71

Tragarle a uno la tierra

(to be swallowed by the earth)
to disappear into nowhere

A: ¿Qué sabes de Alfonso? Hace meses que no sé nada de él. Es como si **le hubiera tragado la tierra.**

B: Tienes razón. Sé que tenía muchos líos. El negocio que tenía le fue muy mal y debía dinero a todo el mundo. A mí todavía me debe un dineral.

A: Teniendo en cuenta sus deudas, no me sorprende que **haya desaparecido.** Ojalá le vaya mejor.

B: ¡Ojalá! Así puede pagar a sus acreedores, que somos muchos.

Quien no se arriesga no pasa la mar

(one who does not take risks, does not pass the sea)
nothing ventured, nothing gained

A: Me han dicho que te vas de la empresa.

B: Me voy mañana. He decidido montar una oficina en mi casa y voy a trabajar independientemente.

A: ¡Qué valiente eres!

B: Pues mira. **Quien no se arriesga no pasa la mar.** Trabajar tantas horas en la oficina no conducía a nada. Ni me dieron un ascenso este año. Si consigo más clientes, voy a ganar muchísimo más trabajando por mi cuenta. Estoy decidido a **correr el riesgo** y, así, salgo adelante.

A: ¡Suerte!

Como pez en el agua

(like a fish in the sea)
to be in one's element

Hacía tiempo que Isabel no había vuelto a su país de origen. Había vivido tantos años en el extranjero que pensaba que le iba a costar acostumbrarse a su país de nuevo. Pero después de tan sólo tres días estaba encantada con todo: la gente, el idioma, las costumbres, la comida y todo lo que le rodeaba. En fin, **estaba completamente a gusto.** Estaba **como pez en el agua.**

Estar entre dos aguas

(to be between two waters)
to be undecided

No sé dónde pasar las vacaciones. Mi prima me invitó a su casa al lado del mar y una gran amiga mía me invitó a su casa cerca de un pequeño lago en las montañas. **No puedo decidir** adónde ir. **Estoy entre dos aguas,** tanto figurativa como literalmente.

Agua pasada no mueve molino

(fallen water doesn't move a mill)
that's water over the dam

A veces María se pone pesadísima. Recuerda todas las faenas que la gente le ha hecho y se pone de mal humor. Parece que no es capaz de **olvidar el pasado y perdonar.** El otro día me dijo que todavía recuerda la tarde que le hice perder su avión porque la recogí tarde. ¡Y eso fue hace seis años! Le dije que **agua pasada no mueve molino,** pero no sirvió para nada.

Parecerse como dos gotas de agua

(to look like two drops of water)
to be like two peas in a pod

Pedro y Pablo son grandes amigos. Tienen los mismos gustos: les encantan los deportes, la música clásica, el cine francés, la política, las novelas rusas, el ajedrez y la comida china. Incluso su manera de hablar, vestir y cortarse el pelo es similar. Muchos creen que son gemelos porque **son casi idénticos. Se parecen como dos gotas de agua.**

Mandar al quinto pino

(to send to the fifth pine tree)
to send to blazes

Ayer por la mañana un vendedor llegó a casa de Paco y trató de venderle una aspiradora. Paco le dijo que no tenía interés y el hombre se fue. Por la tarde, el mismo vendedor llegó otra vez y trató de venderle la aspiradora de nuevo. Paco dijo que no y le cerró la puerta en la cara. Hoy por la mañana, el tipo llegó de nuevo "para darle otra oportunidad". Paco se enfureció y **lo mandó al quinto pino.** Estaba muy cansado de las constantes molestias y por eso **le dijo que no quería verlo nunca más.**

Santos y pecadores

Saints and Sinners

Un viento de mil demonios

(a wind of a thousand demons)
a howling gale

A: ¿Adónde vas?

B: Tengo una cita con Enrique a las tres. Vamos a tomar su velero y navegar en la bahía hasta el Cabo Rojo.

A: ¿Pero no has oído el pronóstico del tiempo para hoy? Dicen que va a hacer **un viento de mil demonios** en la Bahía esta tarde.

B: No lo sabía. Gracias por decírmelo. Le avisaré a Enrique. Él tampoco querrá salir si existe la probabilidad de **un viento violento.**

Alzarse con el santo y la limosna

(to take off with the saint and the alms)
to clear off with everything

Alquilo apartamentos amueblados en el centro y generalmente no tengo problemas con los inquilinos. Siempre me pagan a primeros del mes. Pero recientemente un joven empezó a pagarme con dos o tres semanas de retraso. La situación iba de mal en peor, ya que a finales de la semana pasada me debía dos meses de alquiler. Después de muchas llamadas telefónicas, decidí ir al apartamento y exigirle lo que me debía. Como nadie abrió la puerta, usé mi llave para entrar y me di cuenta de que el chico **se había alzado con el santo y la limosna. Llevó todas sus pertenencias y todos los muebles** del apartamento **y desapareció.**

Andar de Herodes a Pilato

(to walk from Herod to Pilate)
to go from bad to worse

El año pasado decidimos pasar las vacaciones tranquilamente en las montañas. Fuimos en coche y disfrutamos los dos primeros días fabulosamente, pero el tercer día las cosas **fueron de mal en peor.** Primero, se nos reventaron tres llantas. Después, nos falló el motor. Mientras estaban arreglando el coche, dimos un paseo y nos atracaron por el camino. Cuando volvimos al hotel, descubrimos que alguien nos había robado las maletas. ¡Ese viaje sí que **anduvo de Herodes a Pilato!**

Tener ángel

(to have an angel)
to have charm, be charming

A: ¿Qué tal la nueva profesora de inglés?

B: Estamos muy felices con ella. Está muy preparada y explica hasta la gramática más aburrida y difícil de forma original y clara. Sus clases son fantásticas. Aparte de todo esto, la mujer **tiene ángel**. **Es una persona encantadora** e inteligente.

Quedarse para vestir santos

(to stay dressing saints)
to remain an old maid

Salí de mi pueblo a los dieciocho años porque de los cuatrocientos habitantes, trescientos eran mayores de sesenta y cinco años, ochenta y cinco eran mujeres o niños y quince eran hombres casados. Como no quería **quedarme para vestir santos,** me fui a la capital a estudiar y conocer chicos de mi edad para casarme algún día. No quiero **quedarme solterona.**

Hacer su santa voluntad

(to do one's holy will)
to do as one pleases

Ana no hace caso a nadie. Es una mujer de carácter muy fuerte y siempre **quiere imponer su voluntad.** Pero desde el día que llegó Marta, nuestra nueva colega, Ana no tiene más remedio que tener un poco de paciencia. Ya no **hace su santa voluntad** por la oficina mientras está Marta, ¡la hija de los dueños de la empresa!

Aquello fue llegar y besar el santo

(that was arriving and kissing the saint)
it was like taking candy from a baby

Los dos ladrones se estaban felicitando el éxito de su atraco más reciente. Tenían un método infalible: a través de su "contacto" en una agencia de viajes, sabían qué familias estaban de vacaciones. Según ellos, **era facilísimo** entrar en una casa desocupada y llevarse todos los objetos de valor. Pero mientras el uno comentaba al otro que **aquello fue llegar y besar el santo,** entró la poli y los llevó al calabozo. Lo que no sabían los ladrones es que en la última casa que robaron, los dueños habían instalado una cámera. Los dos delincuentes salieron retratados en una pantalla y fue muy fácil identificarlos.

Tener el santo de espaldas

(to have the saint with his back turned)
to be unlucky

Hoy **he tenido mala suerte.** Me desperté tarde y mi coche no
arrancó. Llegué tarde a la oficina y mi jefe me echó una bronca. Luego
se me cayó el café por encima de un informe de treinta páginas y tuve
que sacar otra copia. No comí nada al mediodía porque había dejado la
comida en casa y no traje dinero conmigo. Por la tarde me llamaron
para decirme que habían cancelado el crucero que pensaba hacer el
mes que viene. Cuando salí a las cinco estaba lloviendo y no tenía
paraguas. Cuando llegué al coche me di cuenta de que alguien me
había hecho un tremendo arañazo en la puerta. Llegué a casa sin
novedades, pero a los veinte minutos hubo un apagón y estuve sin luz
toda la noche. Hoy creo que **tenía el santo de espaldas.**

Todos los santos tienen novena

(all saints have novenas)
one's time will come

A nuestro hijo le gusta el baloncesto, pero es el chico más bajito del equipo. Los demás le llevan la cabeza. Las poquísimas veces que consigue agarrar el balón, se lo quitan en seguida. Pasa casi todo el tiempo sentado en el banco, observando a sus compañeros. Lo quiero animar y le digo que algún día crecerá y podrá convertirse en un jugador extraordinario. Mientras tanto, puede participar en otros deportes en los cuales la estatura no figura. Le digo que **todos los santos tienen novena,** y que **algún día él se acomodará** al deporte ideal.

Más feo que el pecado

(uglier than the sin)
as ugly as sin

A: Marta, creo que me está persiguiendo un hombre. Tengo miedo.

B: ¿Quién es? Hay tanta gente en la calle.

A: ¿No ves a uno pequeñito, calvo, flaco y paliducho? Es **feísimo** y tiene la cara llena de granos. Lleva gafas gordas, una gabardina sucia y de color extrañísimo, un calcetín rojo y otro blanco, zapatos de tenis verdes, un paraguas (aunque hace sol), y va con una radio pegada al oído. No quiero dar la vuelta para señalártelo, pero no lo vas a confundir con nadie. Es **más feo que el pecado.**

B: ¡Claro que lo veo! Es Juan. ¡Y es mi novio!

Section Eight

Así es la vida

That's Life

Venir con músicas

(to come with musics)
to tell tall tales

A: Me encontré con Ramón ayer y me contó que había ganado la lotería.

B: Ese Ramón siempre **viene con músicas.** La semana pasada me dijo lo mismo, pero el hombre sigue viviendo en esa casucha y se viste con ropa de segunda mano. ¡Y me debe mucho dinero!

A: ¡Qué mentiroso! Yo no sabía que **él inventaba esas historias.**

Ir por lana y volver trasquilado

(to go for wool and come back shorn)
to get burned

A: Carlos, ¿qué tal? Hace años que no te veo. ¿Cómo va tu negocio?

B: No muy bien, Pedro. **Fui por lana y salí trasquilado.**

A: ¿Qué te pasó?

B: Bueno, quería vender autos grandes y lujosos, pero después de invertir toda mi plata en la compra de doscientos coches, estalló la crisis petrolera y hubo escasez de gasolina. Durante seis meses, nadie quería comprar un coche que usara mucha gasolina, y **perdí todo.**

Cantar de plano

(to sing clearly)
to spill the beans

Ayer arrestaron a Fernando porque sospecharon que él fue el ladrón que había robado el banco. Lo interrogaron durante seis horas sin lograr que confesara, pero cuando le dijeron que su acómplice, Marcos, ya **había confesado todo** culpándole a él, empezó a **cantar de plano.** Claro, después supo que Marcos no les había dicho nada a los policías.

No poder ver a alguien ni en pintura

(not to be able to see someone even in a painting)
not to be able to stand the sight of someone

A: Si puedes, ven a casa a cenar el sábado a las nueve. Vamos a celebrar la publicación de mi nuevo libro.

B: Encantada. ¿Quién más va a estar allá?

A: Bueno, mi editor, dos periodistas, la señora Estrada...

B: ¡¿La señora Estrada?! Entonces, no voy. **No puedo verla ni en pintura.**

A: No sabía que **la odiabas tanto.** ¿Por qué?

B: Porque le dieron el trabajo que me habían prometido en el periódico y se ha convertido en la directora de mi departamento. ¡Me hace la vida imposible!

Fumarse una clase

(to smoke oneself a class)
to skip a class

A: Oye, Juanita, ¿te apetece ir conmigo al cine esta tarde?

B: Me encantaría, pero tengo clase de informática.

A: ¿Y no podrías **fumarte la clase** hoy?

B: ¡Qué va! No puedo **faltar** ni una sola vez, porque la profesora pasa lista y me va a bajar la nota final si falto de nuevo.

Decirle a alguien cuatro verdades

(to tell someone four truths)
to give someone a piece of one's mind

A: ¡Estoy harto! Llevo más de un año sufriendo bajo este nuevo director y no aguanto más.

B: ¿Qué hizo ahora?

A: Critica todo lo que hago, me obliga a hacer todo su trabajo, me pone
cinco tareas a la vez y me grita porque no termino ni con la
primera. ¡Basta ya! Voy a **decirle cuatro verdades.**

B: Hazlo. **Dile lo que piensas de él.** Te acompaño.

A: Bueno...no tengo prisa y no quiero arrepentirme después. A fin de
cuentas, gano mucho aquí.

Destornillarse de risa

(to become unscrewed with laughter)
to split one's sides laughing

Hace poco mi primo Carlos estrenó como hombre del tiempo en la televisión. Toda la familia se reunió delante de la televisión para verlo. Estaría algo nervioso porque cuando tenía que señalar la capital del estado, se equivocó y señaló un lago de un estado vecino. Luego confundió la temperatura en las montañas con la de una playa al sur del país. Después anunció que el récord para temperaturas se había registrado en el año 110 cuando marcó 1,927 grados. Cuando bajaron el mapa, se le cayó encima y Carlos pronosticó un terremoto. **Nosotros nos destornillamos de risa** y parece que algunos directores de la estación también. Carlos ya no es el hombre del tiempo, porque le han dado su propio programa de comedia y le va fenomenal. Ahora **todos se ríen muchísimo** de él.

Tener un tornillo flojo

(to have a loose screw)
to be crazy

Javier tiene una nueva moto y la maneja como si **tuviera un tornillo flojo.** Se pone de pie en el asiento, maneja con las rodillas y, a veces, maneja con los ojos cerrados. ¡Nunca he visto a un joven **tan loco** en toda mi vida!

No saber ni papa de

(not to know even a potato about)
to know nothing about

Mario siempre trata de impresionar a las muchachas. Ayer le dijo a Carmen que es experto en buceo. En realidad **no sabe ni papa de** buceo, pero como Carmen quiere aprenderlo, él le contó su mentirita para impresionarla. Más tarde, Carmen va a darse cuenta de que Mario **no sabe nada...** ¡porque él se va a ahogar tratando de enseñárselo!

Costar un ojo de la cara

(to cost an eye of the face)
to cost an arm and a leg

A: ¿Qué tal las vacaciones?

B: ¡Estupendas! Estuve en Lisboa, Madrid, París, Berlín y Viena.

A: ¡Qué bien!, pero te **habrá costado un ojo de la cara,** ¿no?

B: Pues no **gasté mucho.** Fui de negocios a Lisboa, así que la compañía pagó el viaje. Luego aproveché un fin de semana para ver la ciudad. Compré un pase especial de ferrocarril y salí para Madrid, donde vive mi hermana y me quedé con ella. Luego fui a casa de mi primo en París, a casa de mi cuñado en Berlín y por fin a casa de unos tíos en Viena. Nadie me dejó invitarles ni siquiera a un café. Apenas gasté dinero.

Quemarse las pestañas

(to burn one's eyelashes)
to burn the midnight oil

A: ¿Qué tal va tu clase de químicas?

B: No muy bien. Si no saco una nota decente en el examen mañana, me van a suspender.

A: Supongo que vas a **quedar estudiando toda la noche.**

B: No tengo más remedio. A ver si hago un gran esfuerzo y le deslumbro al profesor. Voy a **quemarme las pestañas**...¡así el profe no me quema vivo mañana!

Perder los estribos

(to lose the stirrups)
to lose one's temper, to fly off the handle

Nuestra vecina es tremenda. **Protesta y se enfada** por cualquier cosa: si ponemos la radio demasiado fuerte, si nuestro perro pisa su precioso jardín, si no cortamos el césped o si lo cortamos por la mañana y la despertamos. Es una mujer que **pierde los estribos** por tonterías. Pero la tratamos muy bien y nunca protestamos. ¡Su marido es el jefe de policía de nuestra ciudad!

Faltarle a uno un tornillo

(to have a screw missing)
to be nuts

A: Paco, mi profesor de historia dice cosas absurdas en la clase.

B: ¿Qué dice?

A: Asegura que Hitler no murió en la Segunda Guerra Mundial. Dice que vive en Paraguay donde está levantando un ejército para conquistar toda América Latina. También nos dijo que Elvis vive en una isla cerca del Triángulo de las Bermudas.

B: Parece que **se ha vuelto completamente loco,** ¿verdad?

A: Sí, creo que **le falta un tornillo.**

Translations
Traducciones

---

1. (page 1)

A: Did you hear that they're going to have to get rid of all the trees in the main square?

B: Why?

A: Because the mayor's wife can't see what her neighbors are doing in their homes with the trees there. So the city is going to cut them down so that the old gossip can spy on her neighbors better.

B: But can she do that?

A: Sure, she's the one who **rules the roost** around here, so she can do whatever she wants. The great thing is that once they cut the trees down, we'll all be able to see what *she's* doing, too!

---

2. (page 2)

A: Hi, Héctor. How's my favorite neighbor?

B: Fine, thanks. How are you doing, Jorge?

A: I'm really happy to see you looking younger than ever, Héctor. How do you do it? And your dear family. The most beautiful wife in the neighborhood, the most obedient and studious children. Your life is just a dream, Héctor. You're the luckiest man I know.

B: Just a minute, Jorge. All you need to do is praise my dog! Look, **I know what your little game is.** I already know that your dog killed my cat, your wife wrecked my car, and your son hit my son. Just stop the false compliments. Besides, I've always hated that cat. The car isn't mine, it belongs to my brother-in-law, and my son deserved it!

3. (page 3)

A: Honey, are we on the right road? We left home more than three hours ago and we're still not at Mom's yet.

B: Of course, dear. I'm taking a new route so that we can see the beautiful countryside.

A: But love, we're going south and Mom's house is north of us. Look, the sun is setting on the right.

B: That's just the reflection of the sun, darling. We're heading north towards the home of my dear mother-in-law.

A: You never **admit it when you're wrong,** Luis. You know you're going the wrong way, but you don't want to admit your mistake. It's just that you don't want to see Mom.

B: On the contrary! I want to see your mother so much that I'm willing to stay on this route until we get there, even if we have to go around the world!

---

4. (page 4)

A: Hi, Pedro. Is it true that the boss named you vice-president?

B: You bet, Manuel! He and I are great friends now.

A: But how did you manage that?

B: Well, since the boss thinks he's the funniest man in the world, I learned to laugh at his jokes.

A: How could you? He tells the worst jokes in the world...and he doesn't know how to tell them.

B: But I've learned **to force a laugh,** and I've gained his confidence. When I have to make myself laugh, I just think about how ridiculous he looks doing it, and I break out laughing.

---

5. (page 5)

My friend, Susana, who is the author of various works for the theater, invited me to the first performance of her latest work, "One Hundred Years of Density," today, September 14. When I arrived at the theater, I got the surprise of my life. **There was hardly anyone** there. Almost no one had come. It seems that Susana is an excellent playwright, but as an editor of promotional brochures, she leaves much to be desired, especially in pinning down the date of the first performance...the fifteenth!

6. (page 6)

In a soccer game against its number one rival, our team played very badly at the beginning of the first half. I don't know what the coach said to them during half-time, but when the kids came back to play, **they really brought it off,** and won 4 to 2.

---

7. (page 7)

A: Well, we've finished dinner and it's just nine-thirty. Where should we go now? To a movie?

B: No, I can't go anywhere. I'm very tired and I'm usually asleep around now.

A: Don't tell me that you go to bed so early.

B: That's right. I like **to go to bed very early** and get up when the roosters start to crow.

---

8. (page 8)

The boss asked me to fire Juanita. She wasn't doing her job well and somebody had to tell her. I talked to her best friend, Ángela, because I wanted her to solve the problem for me. I asked her to tell Juanita that another company was looking for a receptionist and that it would be better if she went there. Ángela told her, and did it so well, that Juanita left very happy. When my boss found out, he called me into his office.

A: Carlos, I asked you to talk to Juanita. Why did Ángela do it?

B: Well, boss, it's always helpful **to pass the buck,** especially if the one receiving it is the best friend of the person in question. Don't you agree?

A: You're absolutely right, Carlos. You've got executive qualities in you, son.

B: Thank you, sir.

A: And Carlos, make sure that the one who really took care of that "buck" gets a good bonus with her paycheck this month...the one you would have received!

---

9. (page 9)

They guided us through the caverns until we arrived at a spot deep inside the big cave. There the guide asked us to extinguish all lights and **it was pitch dark.** You couldn't see a thing, not even your hand in front of your face. I had never experienced such total darkness and it scared me a little. But a few minutes later, when they turned on the lights, we all felt better.

---

10. (page 10)

We wanted to buy a puppy for our daughter. I called a man who had placed an ad in the paper and we decided to meet that night in the parking lot of a closed restaurant. When I got there, he was already selling a dog to a young man. I noticed that he had parked in the darkest part of the lot, and I started to have my doubts. When I saw the dog that the young man had bought, I realized that the poor animal had mange, but it wasn't too notice-able in the dark. We left without speaking to the guy because **we had had a narrow escape.** He almost cheated us, but we saw the trick in time.

---

11. (page 11)

A: Manolo, come here. We're going to the dentist.

B: But Mom, I don't want to go. My girlfriend is here and I don't want to leave her alone.

A: She can stay with your brother. He can talk to her while we're gone. Let's go.

B: But you don't understand, Mom. That would be like **putting the fox in charge of the henhouse.** Juan wants to take her away from me. I can't just leave her with him.

A: OK, then tell Juan to come to the dentist and you stay at home. After all, it's better, now that you have a girlfriend, that you don't see that young woman who works for Dr. Soto.

B: Just a second, Mom. Maybe I should trust Juan...

---

12. (page 12)

A: Pedro, why are you so sad?

B: Well, I just ran into Javier. Some time ago, he loaned me some money and today he told me **to cough up the dough** right away.

A: That seems fair.

B: But giving him the cash really bothered me, because I wanted to buy a nice gift for my girlfriend's birthday. After paying back Javier, I'm left without a dime.

---

13. (page 13)
I told the new students not to talk during the exam, but I didn't expect the absolute silence they maintained for the 50 minutes of the exam. **You could have heard a pin drop.** I was very impressed and decided to tell them to study their Spanish for three hours a day to see if that would bring the same result.

---

14. (page 14)
A: Good morning, sir. I have the pleasure of informing you that you can win a million pesos.
B: How?
A: It's very simple. When you buy this excellent set of encyclopedias, we are going to include your name in our great drawing for a million pesos. All you have to do is sign...
B: **Don't give me that!** You're not going to fool me with that trick. I don't need any encyclopedias. Good-bye!

---

15. (page 15)
A: Luis, what are you doing with those flowers in your hand?
B: I'm waiting for Carla. She invited me for dinner and she said she'd come by for me at seven, but it's nine now.
A: I think **she stood you up.** She's always very punctual. I'm sure she's not going to go out with you. Maybe she found someone who was more handsome, don't you think?
B: Thanks for the encouragement!

---

16. (page 16)
There was a terrible scandal last month. It seems that the Secretary of Transportation was getting bribes from a bus company so he would give them important contracts. They gave him a yacht and a lot of cash, but when the police started to investigate the matter, the Director of Railroads was the one who **got railroaded.** One morning, the yacht "appeared" behind the Director's house, and he was labeled guilty in all the papers. The Director insisted

that he practically gets sea sick taking a bath. He claimed that he doesn't even know how to sail, but no one believed him and he was fired. Days later, the Secretary's house was destroyed by a bomb. They never found out who did it, but someone had left an anchor where the Secretary's bathtub used to be!

---

17. (page 17)

Two medical investigators worked for years on a project to find a drug that would cure obesity. Isabel, the quiet laboratory genius, discovered the formula for creating the drug, but Jorge, her extroverted colleague, manufactured it and promoted it. When the representatives from the Nobel Committee interviewed him about his great discovery, Jorge **looked out for number one.** He didn't even mention Isabel. He accepted all the praise as if he had done everything himself, taking full advantage of the situation. Six months later, when patients started to complain that their hair was falling out, Jorge tried to say that the formula was Isabel's, but no one believed him and he was ruined in the scientific community. Later, Isabel perfected the formula and became a multimillionaire. Today, Jorge is her chauffeur!

---

18. (page 18)

A: Our soccer team is terrible. We'll never win a game.
B: Don't be such a pessimist. We'll get lucky soon, play a really bad team, and win.
A: It would have to be a team of blind men. If not, I think we'll only win **when pigs fly.**
B: You might be right. Maybe we'll never win, but who knows? Maybe we'll win the old-timers' championship in another thirty years…we play like old guys already!

---

19. (page 19)

A: Hi, Pepito. Why are you crying?
B: Mom's going to be away for a whole week and I miss her. That's why I'm so sad.
A: But you shouldn't be **broken-hearted** just because she's not going to be here for a week. She'll be back soon and she'll ask me how you behaved. What do you want me to tell her? That

you spent the whole week crying like a baby or that you behaved like a big boy?

B: Well, if that's going to keep her from taking any more trips, you can tell her that my tears caused a real flood!

---

20. (page 20)

Ana lost her job last year. She wasn't worried because she had a fine education, a lot of experience, and excellent training in her field. She answered a lot of want ads, went to many interviews, but nothing happened. After six months of looking for work without success, **she became discouraged.** It's hard enough to find a good job these days. It could discourage anyone. I hope she gets something soon or she's going to have to accept some mediocre employment just to get by.

---

21. (page 21)

The police were already suspicious about Enrique with respect to some armed robberies in the neighborhood, but they couldn't catch him red-handed. One day, a young police officer passed himself off as a jewelry salesman. When Enrique came in the store and took out his knife to rob him, the policeman pulled out his gun and took Enrique to jail. He had caught him right in the act of robbery.

---

22. (page 22)

Television, radio, newspapers, and magazines bombard us with commercials. Each company promises that its product guarantees happiness, success, and popularity. But after hearing all the claims, seeing all the photos, and listening to the endless promotions, it often seems that they only want to **fill our heads with empty talk.** I'm sure their products aren't as special as they're made out to be. They just want to convince us with empty arguments that don't make sense. Will using this shaving cream make you more attractive? Will wearing a certain cologne make you more romantic? Will using a certain toothpaste make you the world's greatest lover? I doubt it! They're all impossible promises to keep.

23. (page 23)

A: Paco, why are you pestering me? I told you that I didn't want to play tennis today. Stop hitting me with that racquet.

B: But there's no one else to play with, José. You have to play. Either I'll hit the ball in a match with you, or I'll keep hitting you.

A: Paco, **you're really making me lose my temper.** Stop bothering me, or I'll throw this marvelous lemonade in your face.

B: Okay, okay. You don't have to get mad. If you don't want to play, you just have to say so.

---

24. (page 24)

A: Camilo, is my TV ready?

B: No, Mr. Alonso. I'm sorry.

A: But you promised to have it ready today.

B: I know I did, but **I hit a snag,** Mr. Alonso. The part didn't come in.

A: Why not?

B: Well, my brother-in-law brings me the parts and he's very lazy, sir. He's the reason there are so many unexpected delays.

A: Why don't you just fire him?

B: Well, sir, my wife says that if he doesn't have a job, he'll have to come and live with us, and that's something I couldn't put up with!

---

25. (page 25)

A: Enrique, you're my best friend. I want to ask you some advice. You know I'm shy, especially when it comes to talking to women. I know a beautiful and charming woman by the name of Alicia. We met three weeks ago and I think I'm in love, but I don't know how to tell her. What should I do?

B: I think the best thing to do would be **to speak to her from the heart,** Jaime. If you're sure of your feelings for her, you should tell her so sincerely. It could be that she feels the same for you.

110

26. (page 26)

Something strange happened to me yesterday. I was walking down the street when a man came up to me and asked if I wanted to buy a watch. I said, "What watch?," and he rolled up his sleeve to show me about twenty watches that he had on his arm. **My suspicions were aroused** immediately. And when he said that all of them were specially priced at only ten dollars, my suspicions were confirmed. At this point, a policeman passed by, saw the watches, and tried to arrest the guy. The fellow ran away. At least I wasn't buying one of those watches when the police came by!

---

27. (page 27)

A: What do you think about our new boxer, "Alex the Assassin"?
B: He's great! I've never seen anyone who **could hold a candle to him.** He's the best.
A: Well, I agree that he's the best I've ever seen, but I haven't seen the Cuban. They call him "Miguel the Thug."
B: Right, but pretty soon they're going to be calling him "Miguel the Rug" after Alex gets done with him.

---

28. (page 28)

A: Yesterday was April Fool's and we had a lot of fun with Juan, the champion swimmer.
B: Is that right? What did you do to him?
A: You know that Juan never lets one day go by without swimming in the ocean. He claims it's his "champion's promise." He's very proud of his achievements. So we told him that some sailors had seen a shark in the bay.
B: Ah, but **you were just pulling his leg!** Didn't he realize that you were joking?
A: I don't think so. Anyway, we were listening when he told his girlfriend that he wasn't going to go swimming tomorrow because he had been getting cramps and he needed to let his muscles rest for a few days. We laughed like crazy!

29. (page 29)

A: Good morning. Is my car ready?

B: Yes, sir, and we've taken care of everything: the brakes, the tires, the accelerator, and the oil change.

A: What kind of tires did you give me, the regular XBs or the special JXs?

B: The special ones, sir, just like you said.

A: And the brakes, did you tighten them properly?

B: Yes, sir, just like you said.

A: And when you fixed the accelerator, did you put in a regular cable or one with reinforced steel?

B: Really, sir, there's little difference. They're the same.

A: Don't tell me that you used regular cable! I can't stand incompetence! Why didn't you use the steel?

B: Sir, I think you're **nitpicking.**

A: That might be true, but I always like to pay attention to details.

---

30. (page 30)

A: How did the negotiations come out, Madam Ambassador?

B: Well, it was going very well for us until one of my assistants made a mistake and mentioned the border problems between our countries. Since it's a very sensitive issue, they were about to cancel everything.

A: What could you do, Madam Ambassador, to save the meeting?

B: It was difficult. I had **to tread on thin ice** for a while, but soon things calmed down and we could proceed with the negotiations.

---

31. (page 31)

Luisa wrote a script for a movie entitled "The Stars of the Afternoon." She presented it to all the big American film companies, but without success. The work had cost her a lot of money because of the plane trips from city to city and the nights in hotels, and she didn't have much left. But Luisa had a lot of confidence in her script and she decided **to put all her eggs in one basket** and produce the movie herself. She spent everything she had and got some loans, and the movie was a tremendous success.

32. (page 32)

A: Good morning. You asked me to come to school because . . .

B: To talk about your son, Mrs. Castellón. We've been having some problems with him. It turns out that we found another student's money in your son's jacket. We're not sure, but . . .

A: Ma'am, let's **call a spade a spade.** Are you saying that my son is a thief?

B: Yes, Mrs. Castellón, let's be frank. We believe that your son committed a theft.

---

33. (page 33)

A: How's it going, Alejandro? How's everything?

B: We have another boss now. Mr. Gómez retired.

A: That's too bad! You two were really good friends, weren't you?

B: Yes, and I miss him a lot, but I think the new boss is going to be a good one, too. **I hit it off with him.**

A: Great! It's always good to have a good relationship with the boss.

---

34. (page 34)

A: Have you heard about the famous actress who's accused of killing her director?

B: Of course! They talk about the case all the time on the news and on all the talk shows. They're even showing all her old movies every night! **There's no getting away from her!**

A: You're right. I'm tired of hearing about her day and night. She's everywhere.

---

35. (page 35)

Francisco is driving me crazy. He comes into my office every half hour to talk about some silly personal matter. This morning he came in at nine to talk abut his mother-in-law; at nine thirty to talk about his car; at ten to talk about his kids; and at ten thirty to talk about his dog. When he came by again at eleven, I lost my patience and **I told him to go jump in the lake.** I can't stand any more interruptions at work. That's why I told him to leave.

36. (page 36)

The captain sent Sergeant Molino and Corporal Gómez to the jungle on a dangerous mission. Sergeant Molino gave all the orders, but Corporal Gómez did all the work. Gómez cut down the grass to clear the way and built a bridge in order to cross the river. When two snakes appeared, Gómez killed them, and when a tiger came out of the jungle, it was Gómez who had to frighten it away. And it was Gómez who finally destroyed the enemy's fortification. It was Corporal Gómez who **saved Molino's neck.**

When both men reached Lieutenant López's office, Sergeant Molino received all the glory for the completed mission and not once did he mention Gómez, who had done all the work.

---

37. (page 37)

A: So, what are the election results? Was Mayor Santiago re-elected?
B: I have the results and the mayor **lost.** She lost by nearly two thousand votes.
A: How many people voted?
B: Around 2,300.

---

38. (page 38)

When I was twenty, I started a jazz group with some friends. We called ourselves "The Jazzmen." We put on concerts all over Mexico with huge success, but one day Álvaro, the guitarist, announced that he had decided **to go out on his own.** He left us to start his own career as a soloist.

Today, "The Jazzmen" are famous all over Latin America, but Álvaro is still an unknown. Sometimes it's not worth it to work alone and try to triumph by yourself.

---

39. (page 39)

When Albert arrived at Marcos and Marina's house, the two were already fighting. Albert listened while Marcos accused Marina of being a wet blanket who never wanted to go out, and Marina accused Marcos of always wanting to have things his way. Instead of leaving, Alberto decided **to add fuel to the fire** and commented that he agreed with Marcos, and then invited him to a movie. Marina became furious and ran Alberto out of the house with a well-placed kick. At times it's not a good idea to make a heated discussion worse between husband and wife, especially if the wife is stronger than you are!

---

40. (page 40)

A: Hi, Dad. You look great today with that new shirt. It's your color. Or could it be that you've lost some weight? You look so handsome.

B: Thank you, dear.

A: Dad, my girlfriends aren't as lucky as me. Their fathers aren't as loving and generous as you. None of them wants to take us to the movies this afternoon...

B: Well, dear, stop all of this nonsense. If you want me to take you to the movies, **get to the point.** Just ask me.

A: Okay, Dad. Will you take us to the movies this afternoon?

B: In one word, Alicia: NO!

---

41. (page 41)

A: Mommy, I want to go to the park...let's go...please, please...

B: That's enough! Okay, we'll go to the park, but wear your jacket. It's cold.

A: I don't want to wear my jacket! I won't wear it, I don't like it.

B: All right, but don't be such a crybaby.

A: *(IN THE PARK)* Mommy, I'm cold. Oh! I'm so cold. I'm freezing to death. Let me have your jacket, Mommy.

B: That's it! That's **the last straw!** We're going home right now. And the next time I tell you to put on your jacket, you'll put it on or we won't go out.

---

42. (page 42)

Isabel was on vacation on a nice Mexican beach. It was July and it was unbearably hot. Isabel was very thirsty, but there wasn't a single place on the beach where you could buy a cold drink. Suddenly she got the idea of opening a small stand where people could drink something cold. Soon her stand "Doña Isabelita" became the most popular spot on the beach. Isabel was very successful and **made a killing.** Since there was no competition, she really pulled in the money.

---

43. (page 43)

Mr. and Mrs. Fernandez invited me to their house the other day. Since they live in the country and the party was on a summer Sunday afternoon, I thought that everyone would be dressed in casual clothes. I put on my jeans, a short-sleeved shirt, and my gym shoes, and went to their house. I was so embarrassed! When I got there I realized that it was a very elegant gathering. All the guests **were dressed to kill.** The men were in ties and wearing their custom-made suits, and the women had on very elegant dresses and were dripping with expensive jewelry. Everyone was well dressed except me. I had a terrible time!

---

44. (page 44)

The two prisoners couldn't stand their lack of freedom or their small and foul-smelling cell any more. They decided to dig an escape tunnel. They worked all night for three weeks. The time finally came to dig the last part of the tunnel and escape, but when they got out of the tunnel they realized **they had gone from bad to worse.** Instead of escaping jail, the tunnel took them to the isolation cell, the only place in the entire jail that was worse than their own!

---

45. (page 45)

My neighbor is driving me nuts. He's always asking to borrow things he never returns, his dog is ruining my flowers, his cat attacks my canaries, and his son goes around hitting mine. I finally decided to tell him exactly what I thought of him and his entire family. I don't know why I never **got it off my chest** before, but when my neighbor opened the door, I suddenly remembered why. He's six foot four, and has arms like a gorilla. I mumbled that I forgot why I had come and I left.

46. (page 46)

A: Marta, how's your new business going?

B: Not very well, Jorge. The competition between ice-cream shops here on the beach is fierce. I don't know what's going to happen to me.

A: But are you making enough to cover your expenses and pay the bank loan?

B: Not really. **I'm on the razor's edge,** Jorge. I'm about to declare bankruptcy at any time. Do you want to help me? You could be my partner.

A: No thanks, Marta. I just wanted to know how things were going. I don't want to get involved in your precarious situation.

---

47. (page 47)

Mr. Borges needed someone to help with the company's management, and Lisa had great hopes of being the assistant he needed. She knew that she would be perfect for this job and wanted to tell Mr. Borges, when he announced that his son would be filling the slot. Since then, Lisa's been **champing at the bit.** She's impatiently waiting to find another chance for a promotion.

---

48. (page 48)

A: Vicente, I need some potatoes. Go to the store and buy me two kilos.

B: But, Mom, **it's raining cats and dogs.**

A: Take an umbrella.

B: But it's raining very hard. Even with an umbrella I'm going to get wet. I'll wait a few minutes until the rain lets up.

A: Okay, but don't wait too long. I need those potatoes for dinner.

---

49. (page 49)

Guillermo is a truck driver and carries lumber from one city to another. Yesterday, his boss was waiting for him at six because he had another important shipment to make at seven. But Guillermo doesn't care about schedules. He took a long time on the way back and didn't come in until nine. You can imagine **the good scolding he got** from his boss, who criticized him and told him he was irresponsible, lazy, and negligent. He told Guillermo that if this happened again, he would have to fire him.

50. (page 50)

Since Lolita turned fourteen a short time ago, she asked her parents if she could now go downtown with her friends on Saturday nights. They gave her permission on the condition that she be home before midnight. Lolita promised that she would, and went out very pleased. But Lolita forgot about the time, and when she looked at her watch it was already two o'clock in the morning. When she walked into the house, she saw her father **with his hands on his hips,** his face all red and smoke coming out of his ears! Now Lolita spends Saturday nights at home remembering how her father looked with his fists on his hips, when she came in so late.

---

51. (page 51)
A: What's the matter with the boss today? He was furious when he got to the office this morning. He screamed at the messenger, really criticized the receptionist, and yelled at his assistant.
B: I think **he's in a bad mood** because they didn't give him the raise he had asked for.
A: I'm sure that's the reason, but his bad mood hardly justifies this behavior.

---

52. (page 52)
A: Thank you, Mrs. Miller, for coming all this way to finalize the details of the contract. I really appreciate it. Would you like some more coffee? And how is your husband? And your chil...?
B: Excuse me for interrupting, Mr. Ocampo, but I didn't come here **to waste my time.** Just like you, I have a lot to do and so little time. So can we get to the contract now?
A: Mrs. Miller, you're not in your country now. You're here with us, and we are of the opinion that spending some time in pleasant conversation before getting down to business is not wasting one's time. To the contrary, it seems that a brusque way of doing business shows a lack of courtesy.
B: Excuse me, Mr. Ocampo. It seems I have a lot to learn. How is your family?

53. (page 53)

A: How are your cases going, Carlitos, or should I call you counselor Carlitos?

B: My first case was horrible. I was up before a judge of the municipal court. I came well prepared, but I got so nervous when I started to speak, **I made a mess of things.** I confused everything.

A: And your client? What happened to him?

B: Well, in spite of the total confusion that I got myself into, the judge didn't find him guilty, so he didn't go to jail. But she warned me to prepare myself better in the future!

---

54. (page 54)

That Javier is an real hypocrite. Two days ago he praised Esteban while Esteban was around, but as soon as he left, Javier **put him down.** He said he was unpleasant, boring, and a liar. But that's the way he is—Javier's always speaking poorly of people when they're not around.

---

55. (page 55)

A: Pepe, what are you doing?

B: I'm changing the oil in Mrs. Ortega's car.

A: But I told you to fix Mr. Jimenez's car first. I promised it for this afternoon.

B: But Mrs. Ortega asked me to do the work now because she's in a big hurry.

A: Look, Pepe, I'm the one who's **running the show,** not Mrs. Ortega. Do what I tell you.

B: Okay, you're the boss!

---

56. (page 56)

Last Saturday, our candidate for mayor, Luis, invited us for lunch in the country in order to thank us for all the work we had done for him. He invited us for one o'clock, and he told us that he'd take care of everything. Well, we all got there at one, but Luis wasn't there. When he finally showed up two hours later, he excused himself by saying that he had had an important meeting and had forgotten all about the lunch. He didn't even bring anything to eat with him and he left right away. We all thought that Luis **was a failure.** If he's not capable of organizing a lunch, what kind of mayor would he make? That day a lot of people lost their confidence in Luis, and a few days later he lost the election.

---

57. (page 57)

A: Listen Miguel, I have some incredible news!

B: About what, Pablo?

A: Do you know Esperanza?

B: Of course I know her. She and my cousin are getting married in June.

A: She's not going to marry anyone in June, because she married her math professor yesterday!

B: **You don't say!** I didn't know anything about this. What a surprise! Who's going to tell my cousin?

---

58. (page 58)

That Pedro is something else! I can never count on him. He always messes up. He was supposed to meet me here at the train station at two. He has the tickets and all the files for the meeting, but **he left me in the lurch** again. The train left and there's not another one until tomorrow. We'll miss the meeting and we won't have a chance for the contract because Pedro hasn't done what he promised. I'm going to have to find another partner.

---

59. (page 59)

I have a colleague who gets angry very easily. If he doesn't agree with something, he explodes. Last week I told him that I couldn't approve his work plan because he was going to be out of the office too much. **He blew his top.** He got so angry that he couldn't talk and he left my office with such a red face that a friend now calls him "tomato" every time he sees him…and that gets him mad too!

60. (page 60)

I have a big problem. My children asked me to take them to the zoo on Saturday. Without thinking about it, I told them that I would. But later my husband reminded me that I had promised to go with him to an art gallery. I'm faced with two difficult choices. If I go to the zoo, I'm in trouble with my husband; if I go to the gallery, my kids will cry. I don't know what to do. **I'm caught between a rock and a hard place.**

---

61. (page 61)

A: Have you seen Mr. Sanchez's son?

B: No, and I don't think we'll see him for a long time.

A: Why? What happened?

B: The young man wanted to go to Hollywood in order to become an actor, but his dad refused to help him. His mother supported him, but Mr. Sanchez was really against the idea. The kid finally got tired of waiting so long and decided **to cut off all contact** with his father, so he left home. I don't think they've even seen each other or talked to each other since that day.

---

62. (page 62)

Eduardo was a mystery for his physics professor. Eduardo never studied, never answered a single question in class, and never turned in his homework assignments, but every time there was an exam, Eduardo got the highest grade. One day the professor finally solved the great mystery when she caught Eduardo reading notes off his shirt sleeve during an exam. When **she uncovered the secret,** she threw him out of class and Eduardo failed the course.

---

63. (page 63)

A: I don't know what to do, Manuel, I've invited Carmen to go out with me twice and she always has an excuse. Do you think it's because she doesn't like me?

B: Just remember that **the game isn't over yet.** I was told that she likes you very much and that she's free on Saturday. Don't give up. You haven't lost her yet.

64. (page 64)

A: Jaime, look at my car!

B: It's great! When did you buy it?

A: Yesterday.

B: Well, drive me home.

A: I can't. I don't have a license.

B: You don't have a license, but you have a car. Isn't that **putting the cart before the horse?**

A: I know I have things out of order, but they were selling the car at such a great price. So I bought it...without a license. I'll learn to drive soon and I'll take you for a ride.

---

65. (page 65)

A: I liked that movie, especially the great scene when the crowd from ancient Rome starts a riot against some soldiers.

B: Yes, the struggle was impressive. Did you notice that the extras they found for the crowd were still wearing their gym shoes?

A: Not really, no.

B: **You must be blind!** You never see anything.

---

66. (page 66)

Luisa left her keys inside her car and didn't want to pay a locksmith. Since the woman **is nobody's fool,** she made an anonymous phone call to the police saying that there was a bomb in a suspicious-looking car (and of course it was her car!). The specialists arrived and were able to open the door. Luisa came by at that moment and asked them what they were doing. She thought she was very clever until one of the policemen saw her keys in the car and realized what had happened.

---

67. (page 67)

Yesterday it was very hot and I took the kids to the beach. Since they were going to charge me five dollars at the lot, I decided to park the car right on the beach to save money. My children and I had a great time, but when we were ready to leave, my tires got stuck in the sand. I asked the kids to push the car while I tried to get it out of there, but **it was pointless.** It just didn't work. I finally had to call the tow truck, and the "parking" cost me fifty bucks!

68. (page 68)

A: What's your daughter going to do after graduation?

B: I don't know. She talks about traveling around the world, writing a novel, or maybe being an actress.

A: She's not very realistic. She seems **to be daydreaming.** My daughter, on the other hand, is enrolled in the university to study medicine. She wants to be a doctor and I believe she'll make it. She's very practical.

---

69. (page 69)

A: How's your new job, Paco? I understand you have a very important position with a leading publisher.

B: Well, the position is important, but the work is awful. I work longer hours than ever—I don't even have time to go out for lunch, my boss is nuts, two employees have left me, and it takes me more than two hours to get to work. As you can see, **it's nothing to write home about.**

---

70. (page 70)

Gloria Castro is the new singing star of Latin America. Her newest hit, "Give Me Your Love," has sold millions of recordings. The press talks about her all the time. Right now, you could say that **all is going well** for her. I hope she can make another recording soon and keep on being successful in her career.

---

71. (page 71)

Last year I went to a secluded island in the middle of the Pacific Ocean. I had been working a lot and I needed to get away from the office and the daily routine. I was looking forward to resting on the beach, with only a couple of good books for company. What a surprise I got when I found out that in the same hotel where I was staying, there were not only some neighbors of mine, but also the accountant from my office and his wife, my dentist, the manager of the travel agency, her husband, and their five children! As my Grandmother used to say: **It's a small world!** But it's too small for my taste—the island paradise had become something familiar and routine.

72. (page 72)

A: What do you hear from Alfonso? It's been months since I've heard from him. It's as if **he's disappeared into nowhere.**

B: You're right. I know he had a lot of problems. His business went down and he owed everyone money. He still owes me a lot of money too.

A: Keeping in mind his debts, it doesn't surprise me that he's disappeared. I hope things go better for him.

B: I hope so! That way he can pay off his creditors, and there are a lot of us.

---

73. (page 73)

A: They told me you were leaving the company.

B: I'm going tomorrow. I decided to set up an office at home and I'm going to free lance.

A: You're so brave!

B: Well, **nothing ventured, nothing gained.** Working so many hours in the office wasn't getting me anywhere. I didn't even get a raise this year. If I get more clients, I'll make much more working on my own. I've decided to take the risk and, that way, I'll come out ahead.

A: Good luck!

---

74. (page 74)

It was some time since Isabel had been in her native country. She had lived abroad for so many years that she thought it would take a while to get accustomed to her country again. But after just three days she was pleased with everything: the people, the language, the customs, the food, and everything around her. In short, she was very happy. **She was in her element.**

---

75. (page 75)

I don't know where to go on vacation. My cousin invited me to her house by the ocean and a very good friend of mine asked me up to her house near a small lake in the mountains. I can't decide where to go. **I'm undecided.**

76. (page 76)

Sometimes Maria is a big bore. She remembers all the mistakes that people have made and that puts her in a bad mood. It seems that she's not able to forgive and forget the past. The other day she told me that she still remembers the afternoon I make her miss her plane because I picked her up late. And that was six years ago! I told her **that was water over the dam,** but it was no use.

77. (page 77)

Pedro and Pablo are best friends. They have the same interests: they love sports, classical music, French movies, politics, Russian novels, chess, and Chinese food. Even the way they speak, dress, and have their hair cut is similar. A lot of people think that they're twins because they're almost identical. **They're like two peas in a pod.**

78. (page 78)

Yesterday morning a salesman came to Paco's house and tried to sell him a vacuum cleaner. Paco told him that he wasn't interested and the man went away. In the afternoon, the same salesman came back and tried to sell Paco the vacuum cleaner once again. Paco said no and closed the door in his face. This morning the guy came by again in order to give Paco "one more chance." Paco was furious and **sent the guy to blazes.** He was very tired of being constantly bothered and that's why he told him he never wanted to see him again.

79. (page 79)

A: Where are you going?

B: I'm meeting Enrique at three. We're going to take his boat and sail in the bay to Cape Red.

A: But haven't you heard the weather forecast for today? They're predicting **a howling gale** in the bay for this afternoon.

B: I didn't know that. Thanks for telling me. I'll let Enrique know. He won't want to sail either if there's a probability of such a strong wind.

80. (page 80)

I rent furnished apartments downtown and I usually don't have any problems with the tenants. They always pay me by the first of the month. But recently a young man started paying me two or three weeks late. The situation went from bad to worse until he owed me two months' rent at the end of last week. After dozens of phone calls, I decided to go over to the apartment in person and demand what was due. Since no one opened the door, I used my key to get in and I realized the man **had cleared off with everything.** He had taken his belongings and all the furniture in the apartment and disappeared.

---

81. (page 81)

Last year we decided to spend a peaceful vacation in the mountains. We drove and really enjoyed the first two days, but on the third day things went from bad to worse. First we had three flat tires. Then the motor conked out. While the car was being repaired, we decided to go for a walk and were robbed on the way. When we got back to the hotel, we discovered that someone had taken our suitcases. Things really **did go from bad to worse** on that trip!

---

82. (page 82)

A: How's the new English teacher?
B: We're very happy with her. She's highly qualified and explains even the most boring and difficult grammar clearly and in her own way. Her classes are fabulous. In addition to all this, the woman **has charm.** She's a pleasant and intelligent person.

---

83. (page 83)

I left my small town when I was eighteen because of the town's four hundred inhabitants, three hundred were past sixty-five, eighty-five were women or children, and fifteen were married men. Since I didn't want **to remain an old maid,** I left for the capital to study and meet guys my age in order to get married someday. I don't want to be a spinster.

84. (page 84)

Ana doesn't pay attention to anyone. She has a very strong personality and she always wants to impose her will. But since the day that a new colleague, Marta, came on board, Ana has no other choice but to show a little patience. Now she doesn't **do as she pleases** while Marta, the owners' daughter, is around!

---

85. (page 85)

The two thieves were congratulating themselves on their most recent robbery. They had an infallible method: through a "contact" at a travel agency, they knew when families were on vacation. According to them, it was very easy to break into an empty house and carry off all the valuables. But while one of them was telling the other that **it was like taking candy from a baby,** the cops came and carted them off to jail. What the robbers didn't know was that in the last house they robbed, the owners had put in a camera. The two delinquents were pictured on a screen and it was very easy to identify them.

---

86. (page 86)

I've had bad luck today. I woke up late and my car wouldn't start. I got to the office late and my boss yelled at me. Then I spilled my cup of coffee on a thirty-page report that I had to recopy. I had to skip lunch because I had left my lunch at home and I didn't bring any money with me. In the afternoon I was told that the cruise I had planned to take next month had been canceled. When I left at five, it was raining and I didn't have my umbrella. When I got to my car I noticed someone had left a big scratch mark on the door. I got home okay, but twenty minutes later there was a blackout and I was without power all night. Today I think **I've been** really **unlucky.**

---

87. (page 87)

Our son likes to play basketball but he's the shortest boy on the team. All the others are a head taller. The few times he gets the ball, it's taken away from him right away. He spends almost all his time sitting on the bench watching his teammates. I want to encourage him and I tell him that one day he'll grow and then he can become a great player. In the meantime, he can play in other sports where height isn't a factor. I tell him **his time will come,** and that one day he'll find his ideal sport.

---

88. (page 88)

A: Marta, I think a man is following me. I'm afraid.

B: Who is he? There are so many people out on the street.

A: Don't you see a bald, skinny, pale little guy? He's very, very ugly and his face is covered with pimples. He's wearing thick glasses and a dirty raincoat that's a really strange color. He has one red sock and one white one, green tennis shoes, an umbrella (even though it's sunny), and he's holding a radio up to his ear. I don't want to turn around and point him out to you, but you can't mistake him for anyone else. He's **as ugly as sin.**

B: Of course I see him! It's Juan. And he's my boyfriend!

---

89. (page 89)

A: I ran into Ramon yesterday and he told me that he had won the lottery.

B: That Ramon is always **telling tall tales.** Last week he told me the same thing, but the man is still living in that little house and he still wears second-hand clothes. And he owes me a lot of money!

A: What a liar! I didn't know that he made up such stories.

---

90. (page 90)

A: How are you, Carlos? I haven't seen you for years. How's your business going?

B: Not very good, Pedro. **I got burned.**

A: What happened?

B: Well, I wanted to sell big luxury cars, but after investing all my dough in buying two hundred cars, the oil crisis hit and there was little gasoline to be had. For six months, no one wanted to buy a car that used a lot of gas, and I lost everything.

91. (page 91)

They arrested Fernando yesterday because they suspected that he was the one who had robbed the bank. They questioned him for six hours without getting a confession, but when they told him that his accomplice, Marcos, had already confessed and had blamed everything on him, Fernando **spilled the beans.** Naturally, later he found out that Marcos hadn't said a thing to the police.

---

92. (page 92)

A: If you can, come over to the house for dinner at nine on Saturday. We're celebrating the publication of my new book.

B: I'd love to. Who else is going to be there?

A: Well, my publisher, two journalists, Mrs. Estrada...

B: Mrs. Estrada? Then I'm not going. **I can't stand the sight of her.**

A: I didn't know you hated her that much. Why?

B: Because she got the job that I had been promised at the newspaper and now she's the head of my department. She makes my life miserable!

---

93. (page 93)

A: Hey, Juanita, would you like to go to the movies with me this afternoon?

B: I'd love to, but I have computer class.

A: And you couldn't **skip class** today?

B: No way! I can't miss a single class, because the teacher takes attendance and she's going to lower my grade if I miss another one.

---

94. (page 94)

A: I've had it! I've been putting up with the new director for more than a year and I can't stand it any more.

B: What did he do now?

A: He criticizes everything I do and makes me do all his work. He gives me five things to do at once, and yells at me when I don't finish the first thing. Enough is enough! I'm going **to give him a piece of my mind.**

B: Do it. Tell him what you think of him. I'll go with you.
A: Well, I'm not in a hurry and I don't want to feel sorry later. After all, I make a lot of money here.

---

95. (page 95)

A short time ago, my cousin Carlos made his debut as a weatherman on TV. The whole family gathered around the television set to see him. He was probably nervous because when he had to point to the state's capital, he made a mistake and pointed to a lake in a neighboring state. Later he confused the temperature in the mountains with the temperature on the beach in the south of the country. Later he announced that the record temperature was 1,927° back in the year 110. When the map was lowered, it fell on top of him and Carlos forecast an earthquake. **We split our sides laughing** and it seems that some of the station's directors did, too. Carlos doesn't do the weather any more, because he's been given his own comedy show and it's going great. Now everyone can laugh a lot at him.

---

96. (page 96)

Javier has a new motorcycle and he drives it as if **he were crazy.** He stands up on the seat, he steers with his knees, and sometimes he drives with his eyes closed. I've never seen such a crazy young man in my life!

---

97. (page 97)

Mario is always trying to impress the girls. Yesterday he told Carmen that he's an expert at snorkeling. He really **doesn't know a thing about** snorkeling, but since Carmen wants to learn, he told her his little lie in order to impress her. Later, Carmen is going to realize that Mario doesn't know a thing…because he's going to drown trying to teach her!

---

98. (page 98)
A: How was your vacation?
B: Great! I was in Lisbon, Madrid, Paris, Berlin, and Vienna.

A: Wonderful, but **it must have cost you an arm and a leg.**
B: Well, I didn't spend very much. I went to Lisbon on business, so the company paid for the trip. Later I took advantage of a weekend to see the city. Then I bought a special railway pass and left for Madrid. My sister lives there and I stayed with her. Next I went to my cousin's house in Paris, then to my brother-in-law's in Berlin, and finally to my aunt and uncle's house in Vienna. No one let me even buy them a cup of coffee. I hardly spent any money.

---

99. (page 99)
A: How's the chemistry class going?
B: Not very well. If I don't get a decent grade on the exam tomorrow, I'm going to fail.
A: I suppose you're going to stay up all night studying.
B: I have no other choice. I'll make a tremendous effort and impress my professor. I'm going **to burn the midnight oil,** so the prof won't burn me alive tomorrow!

---

100. (page 100)
Our neighbor is something else. She complains and gets angry at anything: if we play the radio too loud, if our dog steps on her precious garden, if we don't cut our grass, or if we cut it in the morning and wake her up. She's a woman who **flies off the handle** over nonsense. But we treat her very well and never complain. Her husband is the chief of police of our town!

---

101. (page 101)
A: Paco, my history teacher is saying absurd things in class.
B: What does he say?
A: He claims that Hitler didn't die in World War II. He says that he's living in Paraguay and is putting together an army to conquer all of Latin America. He also told us that Elvis is living on an island near the Bermuda Triangle.
B: It seems that he's gone completely crazy.
A: Yes, I think **he's nuts.**

Idioms Listed by Key Images

Idioms Listed Alphabetically